Small Track Betting

ALSO BY C. N. RICHARDSON

Horse Sense: An Inside Look at the Sport of Kings
(with Bert Randolph Sugar)

Small Track Betting

Pick More Winners Using This Sure-Fire
Eight-Point System of Race Analysis

C. N. Richardson

Skyhorse Publishing

www.skyhorsepublishing.com

10 9 8 7 6 5 4 3 2 1

Library of Congress Cataloging-in-Publication Data
    Richardson, C. N.
    Small track betting / C.N. Richardson.
        p.   cm.
    Includes bibliographical references and index.
    ISBN-13: 978-1-60239-125-3 (pbk. : alk. paper)
    ISBN-10: 1-60239-125-4 (pbk. : alk. paper)
    1. Horse racing—Betting—United States.   I. Title.

  SF332.R53   2007
  798.401—dc22

                                        2007011278

Printed in the United States of America

To my Francesca, who for nearly a quarter-of-a-century has said to me, "You play to win the game. Go with your gut, not against it."

And finally, to my Milan, who believes that winning means a steak dinner and losing means pasta.

Small Track Betting

Contents

CHAPTER ONE

You Want the Money?

PEOPLE HAVE BEEN writing books on wagering for longer than I can remember. But pretty much, they have concentrated on large tracks such as Belmont, Churchill Downs, Santa Anita, Saratoga, or Del Mar. While the major tracks are great, the day-to-day "meat and potatoes" belongs to the regional tracks. And while the major tracks have been busy trying to figure out whether or not they really want to push for legislation to allow video lottery terminals (VLTs) and how much their respective state will take from the "till," I have for the past three years profitably followed four regional tracks:

Finger Lakes Racetrack, Great Lakes Downs, Lone Star Park, and Turf Paradise—these tracks are located in four separate quadrants of the country and operate roughly between April and November, except for Turf Paradise, which operates from October through May. For the most part, this allows you to place your bets on tracks that can offer you the best racing conditions. In the past three years, there have been only four instances when I could not find a fast track in at least one of these locations across the country. But in the event that global warming affects these four I have included two additional track that you might want to look at: Tampa Bay Downs and Turfway Park.

Much of the fun of being a sports fan is testing one's knowledge by making predictions about upcoming events. Wherever fans meet,

from barrooms to boardrooms, talk inevitably turns to friendly argu-
ments about who's going to win "the game tonight," "the fight next
week," "the pennant," etc. More than occasionally, these beliefs are
backed up by a wager or two.

One of the great pleasures of Thoroughbred racing is that the fan
can participate right at the track by matching his hedge against all the
other horses in the pari-mutuel system and wager against other fans,
not against the "house." In contrast to most card games, in which winning depends upon enough luck to beat a fixed-house percentage,
winning at the track can result from forming educated opinions that
are better than average. While the steady rise in pari-mutuel takeout
from 15 percent to 25 percent has changed the criterion for success
from "better than average" to "much better than average," a significant number of horseplayers, relying on keen judgment instead of
luck, can come out consistently ahead over weeks, months, and years.

The way these winners evaluate horse races is exactly the way
opinions are formed by other kinds of experts: doctors, stockbrokers,
baseball managers, lawyers, etc. The process has three stages:

1. **Gathering information**: Forming an expert opinion on a complex subject requires obtaining as much information as possible. A
doctor wouldn't dream of recommending major surgery after only
recording a patient's pulse rate and blood pressure. Horseplayers, on
the other hand, often wager hundreds of dollars on the basis of systems that concentrate on only one or two bits of information, such as
the horse's final time in its last race or its total earnings.

2. **Interpreting information**: To use information properly, a
person has to be taught what it means. For example, learning that a
horse is wearing blinkers for the first time is meaningless if one
doesn't know what blinkers are and why they are used.

3. **Weighing information**: The vital and complex third stage in
forming an opinion is using one's experience to weigh the relative
importance of the information one has gathered and interpreted.

The one thing that is consistent in racing is the plethora of questions that are asked and sometimes even answered. Take for example this question: Will a ten-pound-lower weight assignment, for example, allow a horse to carry its speed a furlong farther than it ever has before? Welcome to the art of weighing all such factors, which together probably determine the outcome of a race; it is called handicapping.

Unfortunately, most race-goers never learn how to play the game of handicapping. The problem is two-fold: First, they lack a large body of important information about the characteristics of horses; and second, they are confronted with an even larger body of information they can't understand, much less evaluate: the past performance charts, results charts, etc. Since few tracks make any attempt to educate their customers, race-goers are left to try to decipher the information on their own or to accept the analysis presented by the house tout. After a few futile and frustrating attempts, most give up the task as "impossible." Or they then revert to such methods as choice of color, lucky numbers, or other such fatalistic prognostications.

This pondering and plodding is in part the reason why the sport has such a high age factor. The fact is that today we have created a universe of instant answers. I find it ludicrous that the average student feels free to acknowledge the delusion that he or she need not learn how to spell, believing that spell check was created to do it for them.

It's bad enough that these psychological failures leave bettors open to a large number of "easy" answers to the problem of how to bet their money. One route is to become a "chalk" player, slavishly following the opinion of the crowd by betting on favorites. Some horseplayers hearken to the conspiracy theory, scrounging for "inside" information, even following trainers and grooms to the betting windows to watch them place their wagers. Still other race-goers simply buy opinions, following the selections of newspaper handicappers, tip sheets, telephone tip services, and touts. Finally, a lot of horseplayers who still hunger to become knowledgeable about the sport succumb to the lavish ads that "guarantee" to teach successful handicapping. In exchange for their $10 to $50, they receive systems into which they're instructed to plug information they still don't fully understand. Buying systems is really the same as buying tip sheets, only a lot more expensive.

Good handicapping doesn't involve relying solely on a mechanical system. Real handicappers, like physicians or financial analysts, develop a systematic approach, weighing the information they've gained and interpreted. Inevitably, just as football coaches have different philosophies, winning handicappers place more weight on certain nuggets of information. Speed handicappers, for example, place special emphasis on the final times of one horse versus another in a given race. While class handicappers judge a horse primarily by the company it's keeping, pace handicappers concentrate on the horse's time and position at various points within a series of past races.

Although the speed handicappers watch final times most heavily, they by no means ignore class, pace, distance, track conditions, weight, or any other single factor. Through experience, these handicappers have realized that the most sophisticated rating of a horse's speed won't help it win if it's entered at the wrong distance, against superior class animals, or on a track it can't handle under deteriorated conditions. Complex judgments cannot be reduced to a few simple rules or systematic manipulations.

Explaining exactly how different kinds of handicappers weigh all the factors that affect the performance of all kinds of horses in different kinds of races is a formidable task that would require many volumes. My purpose in this book is to provide the information racing fans need to become experts on their own. Accordingly, in this section, we're going to concentrate on the first two steps involved in forming an opinion and interpreting the information available to handicappers. While we will go into some detail on handicapping procedures, we also will describe and evaluate those who offer, for a fee, to help you get to stage three—offers that range from touts and tip sheets that provide dubious opinions, to valuable texts by skilled handicappers.

There are eight things that are required in order to follow my system of race analysis:

1. You must know your track.
2. In order to know the track, you must have knowledge of the trainers.
3. You must have knowledge of the jockeys.
4. As with any form of analysis, you must have the tools necessary, i.e., *Daily Racing Form*, Equibase stats, etc.
5. Unless you can be present, you need to select either a phone or online account for betting.
6. Limit your bets to no more than five races at any given track.
7. Select the types of wager you feel the most comfortable with. In my case, I prefer to choose exotic wagering—exacta, trifecta, and pick threes are my preference—in order to maximize an investment.
8. Set a realistic rate of return.

I have dedicated a whole chapter to each of the six tracks, and I explain and exhibit examples of how these eight requirements have produced my own valued return on investment.

While the eight requirements are mandatory, there are other individual idiosyncrasies: I never bet on a race that I can't see, either on simulcast or live. Even when you lose, you can still learn. You will find that keeping notes that you can refer to later may be extremely helpful when a horse returns to the track. A horse that relieves himself on the track will relieve you of your money. All athletes lie about injuries and jockeys are no different, so keep your eyes open. If shoes make the man, then the same can be said of horses. Wrong shoes don't win right races. And last but not least, weights are assigned for a purpose. With rare exceptions, if a jockey can't make weight, don't bet on him to win.

If you have wagered at any of the East Coast tracks in the past year, you have seen the sign Net Pool Pricing plastered across the screen more times than Ms. Cleo has said "I see a change coming."

Net Pool Pricing means that each jurisdiction taking part in the betting pool usually offers different retention rates (also known as takeout rates). In order to pay out a fair and equitable return on each jurisdiction's bet, the system calculates the exact rate based upon their contribution to the pool. For example, if a participant chooses to use a higher takeout than the host track, they will have proportionately less weighing in the co-mingled pool than wagers with a lower takeout rate. Therefore, jurisdictions using a higher retention offer a lower payout to their customers, and the remainder of the network is not affected. This also would work the other way should the participant use a lower takeout, and their respective prices would be higher than the host track.

Here are the takeout rates for the tracks used in this book:

TRACK	EXACTA	TRIFECTA	SUPERFECTA	PIC 3, 4, 6
Finger Lakes	20.5%	25%	25%	25%
Great Lakes Downs	20.5%	20.5%	20.5%	25%
Lone Star Park	21%	25%	25%	25%
Turf Paradise	22.5%	22.5%	22.5%	22.5%
Tampa Bay	21.5%	25.9%	25.9%	25%
Turfway Park	22%	22%	22%	22%

The state and the track will take their portion of your money before you even see any return on your investment in the chosen race, and there is one other partner that you acquire when and if you win. This is your adopted Uncle Sammy. It should be noted that, in all instances, the winning tickets on all of these bets had a partner. The Internal Revenue Service requires that tax be withheld on payoffs over $600 on a $2.00 bet, or where the odds were 300-1 or more, and when the total payoff is in excess of $5,000. In all cases, the tax rate of 27 percent will be deducted in advance of a payout.

For winnings that exceed 300-1 odds—more than $600—the Internal Revenue Service requires that a W2-G Tax Form be completed. In order to collect your winnings, the track requires two forms of identification: First, a copy of your driver's license; and second, a copy of your Social Security card or a card that establishes your identity and includes your Social Security number.

☐ CORRECTED (if checked)			

PAYER'S name, address, ZIP code, federal identification number, and telephone number	1 Gross winnings	2 Federal income tax withheld	OMB No. 1545-0238
	3 Type of wager	4 Date won	2006
	5 Transaction	6 Race	Form W-2G
	7 Winnings from identical wagers	8 Cashier	Certain Gambling Winnings
WINNER'S name, address (including apt. no.), and ZIP code	9 Winner's taxpayer identification no.	10 Window	This is important tax information and is being furnished to the Internal Revenue Service. If you are required to file a return, a negligence penalty or other sanction may be imposed on you if this income is taxable and the IRS determines that it has not been reported.
	11 First I.D.	12 Second I.D.	
	13 State/Payer's state identification no.	14 State income tax withheld	
Under penalties of perjury, I declare that, to the best of my knowledge and belief, the name, address, and taxpayer identification number that I have furnished correctly identify me as the recipient of this payment and any payments from identical wagers, and that no other person is entitled to any part of these payments.			Copy C
Signature ▶		Date ▶	For Winner's Records
Form W-2G		Department of the Treasury - Internal Revenue Service	

Instructions to Winner

Box 1. The payer must furnish a Form W-2G to you if you receive:

1. $600 or more in gambling winnings and the payout is at least 300 times the amount of the wager (except winnings from bingo, keno, and slot machines);

2. $1,200 or more in gambling winnings from bingo or slot machines;

3. $1,500 or more in proceeds (the amount of winnings less the amount of the wager) from keno; or

4. Any gambling winnings subject to federal income tax withholding.

Generally, report all gambling winnings on the "Other income" line of Form 1040. You can deduct gambling losses as an itemized deduction, but you cannot deduct more than your winnings. Keep an accurate record of your winnings and losses, and be able to prove these amounts with receipts, tickets, statements, or similar items that you have saved. For additional information, see Pub. 17, Your Federal Income Tax, Pub. 505, Tax Withholding and Estimated Tax, and Pub. 525, Taxable and Nontaxable Income.

Box 2. Any federal income tax withheld on these winnings is shown in this box. Federal income tax must be withheld at the rate of 25% on certain winnings less the wager.

If you did not provide your federal identification number to the payer, the amount in this box may be subject to backup withholding at a 28% rate.

Include the amount shown in box 2 on your Form 1040 as federal income tax withheld.

Signature. You must sign Form W-2G if you are the only person entitled to the winnings and the winnings are subject to regular gambling withholding.

Other winners. Prepare Form 5754, Statement by Person(s) Receiving Gambling Winnings, if another person is entitled to any part of these winnings. Give Form 5754 to the payer.

The question that I have always had is, Why does the track ask for a Social Security card when no one else will accept your Social Security card as identification? But the next kick in the chops comes when you notice that the cashiers also subtract that additional 27 to 35 percent for the IRS. The reason for the jump from 27 to 35 percent is what I call the "Me Too Factor (MTF)." The MTF is the rate charged by the state and local authorities that also want in on your winnings.

But like anything else, there are those willing to create a means of evading this procedure. I remember back in the '70s, there was a woman who frequented the New York Racing Association (NYRA) circuit. For the sake of anonymity, let's call her "Rosemary Rosary," since she could be found daily at Aqueduct or Belmont during the racing season seated on a bench near the Cashier's Window with rosary beads in hand. Rosemary was called a "percenter." She made her living out of cashing big winning tickets for gamblers who either had an aversion to the IRS or to a parole officer who thought that the ex-con in question was "gainfully" and not "game fully" employed.

Let's say, for example, you won a trifecta that paid $6,000. If you cashed the ticket, you would collect $4,380 ($6,000 minus $1,620, or 27 percent in taxes) and you would be required to list the transaction on your tax return. For her services, Rosemary would cash the ticket using her Social Security number, then return $4,000 to her clientele and pocket $380.

When it came time to filing taxes, Rosemary didn't have to worry, since she had been picking up $100 discarded losing tickets off the ground after each race. The IRS says you can deduct your losses to the extent of your winnings, and Rosemary had losing tickets as proof to offset her paper gains.

Years later I found out that Rosemary had passed away. It appeared that she did quite well for herself as a "percenter." Her oldest son had graduated from MIT, and he got a job working for a major aerospace company.

Here is an instance when one can say crime doesn't pay, even for criminals. There is the tale of the two dumb "wise guys" from Brooklyn who thought they could bypass Rosemary (the woman in the story above) and save the percentage. These eternal idiots were collectors for a local loan shark in New York's garment district. They were required to turn over the receipts each day at 6 p.m. Having made the collections early, they went to Aqueduct and decided to place a few bets. As fate would have it, they lost their own money and decided to continue playing with the collection money. Their luck didn't change, however, until the last race, when they took a last stab at a trifecta. At this point, the racing gods decided to help the sorrowful by giving them winning tickets that paid more than $24,000.

Having never won that much money before, the two men then attempted to cash the tickets and replace the misspent collections. But they were surprised when the cashier presented them not with cash but with checks for their net winnings. Two days later there was a small article in the *Long Island Press* that read, "Two Dead in Trunk at Airport." The article went on to say that two victims were found with a series of losing tickets, and each had a pair of rosary beads around their necks.

As we have seen, the payout to the bettor can be quite lucrative, but the daily on-track betting pool is also profitable to the track. If one were to look at the on-track total betting handle, usually found at the bottom of the racing results section of your local newspaper, you would see, in capsule form, a rough estimate of the income for a given track for that day. This is because the track makes its money by withholding a percentage from the wagering pool, called the "takeout." This amount can range from 14 percent to 27.5 percent across the nation.

Here is the case of a philanderer who got more than his just rewards. Two years ago while on a tryst up at Saratoga, he won a superfecta that totaled $134,000. This benevolent sugar daddy gave his paramour $20,000 of his winning.

The following April, he told his wife to stop by the accountant's office and sign the tax return. However, as the wife began to peruse its content, she came upon something that she had never seen before, Form 5754. This rather innocuous form is prepared when others share in your winnings. This simple act of, shall I say, kindness gave his wife the ammunition she so desperately had been searching for in her quest for a windfall divorce settlement.

Form **5754** (Rev. August 2005) Department of the Treasury Internal Revenue Service	**Statement by Person(s) Receiving Gambling Winnings** ▶ Recipients of gambling winnings should see the instructions on the back of this form. ▶ Payers of gambling winnings should see the separate instructions for Forms W-2G and 5754.			OMB No. 1545-0238 Return to payer. Do not send to the IRS.
Date won	Type of winnings	Game number	Machine number	Race number

Part I Person to Whom Winnings Are Paid

Name		Address		
Taxpayer identification number	Other I.D.		Amount received	Federal income tax withheld

Part II Persons to Whom Winnings Are Taxable *(continued on page 2)*

(a) Name	(b) Taxpayer identification number	(c) Address	(d) Amount won	(e) Winnings from identical wagers

Under penalties of perjury, I declare that, to the best of my knowledge and belief, the names, addresses, and taxpayer identification numbers that I have furnished correctly identify me as the recipient of this payment and correctly identify each person entitled to any part of this payment and any payments from identical wagers.

Like the chorus goes in the old Kenny Rogers song "The Gambler": "There'll be time enough for counting when the dealing's done." Well, there was the disgruntled ex-husband, who lost, according to his calculations, some 75 percent of his total assets. As for the distraught wife, rumor has it that she was last seen shopping for a new vacation condo apartment in Mexico.

For those of you who are mystified by the general payoffs based upon the odds, here is a schedule of standard payouts based upon track odds:

Win Odds	Minimum Payoff	Win Odds	Minimum Payoff
1-1	$4	6-1	$14
2-1	$6	8-1	$18
5-2	$7	10-1	$22
3-1	$8	12-1	$26
7-2	$9	15-1	$32
4-1	$10	20-1	$42
9-2	$11	50-1	$102
5-1	$12		

Pari-mutuel betting (the term is taken from the French language) is a betting system in which all bets of a particular type are placed together in a pool; taxes and a house-take are removed, and payoff odds are calculated by sharing the pool among all placed bets.

The pari-mutuel system is used in gambling on horse racing, dog racing, and in the game jai alai. It is used in events that have a relatively short duration, whereby participants finish in a ranked order. A modified pari-mutuel system is also used in some lottery games.

Pari-mutuel gambling is frequently state-regulated and offered in many places where gambling is otherwise illegal. Pari-mutuel gambling is also offered at off-track facilities, where players may bet on the events without actually being present to observe them in person.

Pari-mutuel betting differs from fixed-odds betting in that the final payout is not determined until the pool is closed; in fixed-odds betting, the payout is agreed upon at the time the bet is sold.

Exotic wagering over the past twenty years has become a major part of an on- and off-track wagering handle. Each exotic wager has a separate wagering pool that determines the payout. There are several forms of betting in this format. They are:

♣ DAILY DOUBLE
Of all the forms of exotic wagering, the daily double is the oldest form of multiple wagers in racing. The players must correctly select the winners of two consecutive races on a single ticket. There are instances when a bettor really likes one horse in either half of the daily double, and the bettor may wish to "wheel" his/her top selection. All the bettor needs to do when placing the bet with the mutual clerk is to say, "A $2 Daily Double Wheel on three and all"; if the bettor wants the number-three horse in the first half with all starters in the second half, the bet is "a $2 Daily Double Wheel on all and three."

♣ EXACTA
The exacta wager is the second most popular form of exotic wagering. Its roots date back to the early '70s. In the exacta, a bettor is asked to select the first- and second-place finishers in that exact order.

♣ EXACTA BOX

This was a term that was substituted for what the old numbers runners of the '50s called "covering the back door." It allows the bettor to select two horses; regardless of which horse comes in first, you're a winner! So, if you ask for a $2 exacta box on two and four, you then receive a ticket with the combinations of both 2-4 and 4-2. If your top two picks finish first and second, in either order, you win! It costs $4 for a two-horse box, $12 for a three-horse box, and $24 to box four horses.

♣ EXACTA WHEELS

Now let's say you happen to like a particular horse to finish in either first or second place; you can wheel that horse and receive a ticket giving you that horse in either first or second place, with all the other horses in the race.

♣ QUINELLA

In the quinella, you can pick two horses in any order; you will win if these two horses are the first two to finish, regardless of order.

♣ TRIFECTA

In playing a trifecta, you must pick the exact order of finish of three horses in a given race. There is a minimum $2 straight bet on the trifecta. In order to "box" three horses in the trifecta, you will win if the three picks finish first, second, and third, in any order. It costs $12 to box three horses in the trifecta ($3×2×1×$2=12), or $6 for the $1 box; the result provides half the payoff of a full winning ticket.

♣ SUPERFECTA

The superfecta wager is similar to the trifecta. When playing the superfecta, you must pick the exact order of finish of four horses in a given race. There is a minimum $2 straight bet on the superfecta, or $1 on a box. The minimum bet then would be $4×3×2×1×$1$ or $24. A number of tracks have recently introduced the 10-cent superfecta.

Let's say, that you have selected the number-one horse to win, the number-three horse for second, the number-six horse for third, and the number-five horse for fourth place. Ask the mutual clerk for a "$2 superfecta on one, three, six, and five." If the exact order of finish in the race is 1-3-6-5, you win!

♣ PICK 3/DAILY TRIFECTA

Here you must select the winners of three consecutive races with a minimum wager of $2. This would include a single horse in each of the three races. Additionally, the $1 base wagers on wheels or partial wheels are also available.

In a case where no one has picked three winners, then the pool is distributed to the individual(s) who picked any two winners in three consecutive races. If no one has picked two winners, the pool is distributed to the individual(s) who picked one winner in any of the three consecutive races.

Now that you understand the rules and know how to bet, let's clarify your investment. In my case, I chose $40 as my net investment criteria; that is, net of my racing program. At New York City Off-Track Betting, it costs $2.00 and it lists the tracks that I'm going to wager on. I chose $40 because, in the first place, the bet is small enough that you won't miss it, and secondly, it's about the average size of a New York bar tab.

For simplicity's sake, all of my wagers in this exercise are in $1.00 multiples. If you feel that you need to know why I use dollar multiples, it's because that's how I play the slots. The next step is to determine what you would consider a fair rate of return. I've chosen $250 net per day for the following reasons: First, there is the fact that as a banker of twenty-five years (now retired), I have a fair knowledge of a rate of return. Second, I have survived a quarter of a century with the same woman, and the odds of making another twenty-five are about as diminishing as my memories of the flamingos at Hialeah. And third, because, when my bride said, quoting Herman Edwards, the former coach of the New York Jets, "You play to win the game," I did! And last, but not least, with an additional $40k a year, you can buy T-Bills and not worry about Social Security intrigue and pension shortfalls.

As with any other good wagering system, it would be unfair not to offer you a series of disclaimers. While cigarette packaging repeats the Surgeon General's warning that cigarette smoke contains carbon monoxide, I quote Mae West instead and say, "An ounce of performance is worth pounds of promises." So in this book, I have used the races that I have won at each of the tracks mentioned as examples.

CHAPTER TWO

Finger Lakes
Gaming and Racetrack

♣ KNOW YOUR TRACK

Finger Lakes Gaming and Racetrack is located in the middle of the Finger Lakes region of upstate New York. The track was established in 1962, and it has hosted over 60,000 races, with attendance over the years exceeding eighteen million fans. Since 2004, a $10.5 million renovation along with video gaming has taken this facility from a secret in upstate New York to a profitable player on the racing circuit. As of the conclusion of its forty-first season of operation in 2002, the only Thoroughbred track in western New York has combined on-site wagers of over $1.6 billion. Off-track patrons have contributed an additional $2.6 billion to the handle, bringing the all-time wagering total on Finger Lakes racing to over $4.2 billion.

The track is a one-mile oval on a sandy loam surface with a chute for 6-furlong and 1¼-mile races. The length of stretch is 960 feet. While not particularly long, it could be considered mid-range. Because of its size, there are no turf races conducted.

The track does have a few quirks. In discussions with several non-regular jockeys, many have said that the track, at times, does have quite a "heavy, cuppy" feeling. Also, it can develop quite an inside bias several times during the nearly nine-month season.

Track announcer Ross Morton is the consummate professional, and his race calls are crisp and accurate, with neither the gimmicks nor linguistic alliterations that have started to permeate this time-honored profession. I normally have no complaints, but to mention a shortcoming, it would be that he does not announce shoe changes, though he does announce rider weight changes immediately.

Since many of the resident trainers are always on the lookout for mid-range horses, one of the factors that you will see during the season are horses from all up and down the East Coast corridors.

Particular interest should be given to trainers, one of them being Linda Rice, who uses Finger Lakes as a training track before moving her young horses downstate to Belmont and Aqueduct to compete for higher purses. Conversely, local trainers like Michael Ferraro, Anthony Ferraro, Chris Englehart, and James Acquilano have been known to prep horses at Finger Lakes in several $10,000 races and then ship their horses over to Saratoga and walk away with a 20-1 or 30-1 long-shot winner of a $100,000 purse. In fact, if truth were told, last season several owners of half-million dollar horses found being beaten by the Ferraro tandem of $15,000 acquisitions about as funny as a sharp stick in the eye.

Another factor that often goes unmentioned is the feeder track correlations. Since the major job of a trainer is to place his/her younger horses in a race that he/she can both learn and earn from, many times horses are shipped from track to track in search of those two specific factors. There are, however, wide variances in price and condition levels from track to track. Also, in analyzing distance races, the length from the final turn to the finish line is a variable that can make the difference between a winning trifecta and a losing ticket.

Take, for example, a horse that broke his maiden at a distance of one mile, seventy yards. At Belmont, that is a one-turn race over a large track with wide sweeping turns. The same race at Suffolk Downs, let's say, requires navigating two sharp turns. While early positioning is crucial because of the distance from start to the first turn, the final turn difference is critical. At Belmont, the distance from last turn to finish line is 1,097 feet, while at Suffolk, the distance from last turn to the finish line is 1,030 feet. This is even more acute at tracks such as Mountaineer Park, where the distance from last turn to finish line is only 905.31 feet.

In the case of Finger Lakes, the three main tracks that you will frequently see in past performances are Fort Erie, Mountaineer, and Suffolk Downs. Here is a table of factors that I use in my intangible calculations when looking at races at Finger Lakes, where the distance from last turn to finish line is 960 feet.

TRACK	DISTANCE	FACTOR
Fort Erie	5-furlongs	-1
	6-furlongs	-1
	7-furlongs	1
	1-mile	-2
	1-mile 70	-2
Suffolk Downs	5-furlongs	+1
	6-furlongs	+1
	7-furlongs	+2
	1-mile	+3
	1-mile 70	+2
Mountaineer Park	5-furlongs	-1
	6-furlongs	-1
	7-furlongs	1
	1-mile	+1
	1-mile 70	+2

As for the feeder track correlations of price and condition levels from track to track, this has become harder to differentiate with the advent of increased purses brought about by Video Lottery Terminal (VLT) income. I will say that the bottom-priced claimers at Fort Erie, Mountaineer, and Suffolk Downs, however, don't equate equally to those at Finger Lakes.

♣ KNOW YOUR TRAINERS

While another profession has coveted the title of "the world's oldest," horse training is certainly the world's oldest honorable profession. For millennia, from the dawn of civilization to the invention of the internal combustion engine, the horse was mankind's most valuable servant—but the horse was also an animal with a deeply inbred spirit that made bending the animal to man's will a demanding task. That's why the horse trainer had achieved a lofty ranking by the beginning of recorded time, and why treatises on equitation have been found among the earliest known written records.

The job of the modern Thoroughbred trainer, on the surface, is much like that of the manager of a professional boxer. They're sort of like the Angelo Dundee of horse racing. The trainer finds "prospects" to handle, arranges "matches" for them, then he brings his charges to the best possible peak of fitness to meet their opponents. While the basic responsibilities of a trainer can be summarized in a sentence, the infinite variety of races, racing conditions, and racehorses makes the details of the job difficult to summarize in a few paragraphs or pages.

The second and third parts of a trainer's job are equally difficult. One part is the actual process of conditioning the horse. This involves the ability to read minute changes in attitude and health that can translate into poor performance. The second of these jobs is the relationship with the owner. The trainer must balance the needs of the horse with the needs and interests of the owner. Trainers who are the best conditioners in the world will not make money if they can't get along with the people who make the investment in Thoroughbred racing stock.

At every American track, there is a small number of very skilled trainers and a larger number of far less competent trainers. Because of the general lack of coverage of racing by the daily newspapers, trainers are little known to the racing fan.

While the racetrack and racing secretary develop the racing pro-gram and create races, the trainer must choose the program with which to be associated. With an understanding equal to that of the racing secretary, the trainer must interpret the conditions of the races that have been created to determine the best possible races in which to place his charges.

While I have already mentioned that trainers place horses in races that they expect to get something out of and learn from, the record of accomplishment speaks volumes as to their value in the analysis.

There are the horses—not only horses of a different color, but of different levels of skill as well. While some barns suffer an embar-rassment of riches, others are less apt to house a stake horse than a barn full of claimers, more from the Yellow Pages than Blue Book. However, as Hall of Fame trainer John Nerud, who more than once had a horse of questionable lineage, would say, "Don't tell me whom he's by, just tell me whom he's passed."

Here are the leading trainers at Finger Lakes for 2006:

Name	Starts	1st	2nd	3rd	Earnings
Chris J. Englehart	515	129	82	69	$1,221,868
Charlton Baker	287	68	53	47	$1,008,971
Michael A. Lecesse	320	67	47	45	$743,034
Michael S. Ferraro	241	58	48	34	$716,523
Oscar S. Barrera, Jr.	391	57	61	61	$709,995
M. Anthony Ferraro	287	50	43	41	$622,259
James S. Acquilano	279	48	51	43	$475,741
James T. Wright	244	48	43	27	$560,131

♣ KNOW YOUR JOCKEY

The most important thing that a bettor has to do with a jockey is to watch him in action. This more accurately allows you to look at the jockey's standing numbers and see his style of riding, as well as his ability to anticipate danger with the horse in question. There are only two things that any bettor can ask of a jockey—the abilities to anticipate and to evaluate the situation. That is his job, and if he can't do either, then it's better to pass on him or her and look elsewhere. Or to paraphrase the late attorney Johnny Cochran, "If the jockey don't fit, you must a-quit."

A good jockey is one who settles his mount into a rhythm that even the most casual observer can notice. If a jockey is bouncing around on a horse like a pinball machine, then the horse has something else to think about other than running. This flow in unison should be maintained until they reach the top of the stretch, and then the jockey allows the horse to use what energy he has left to try and get to the finish line either first or as close to first as he can.

To a trainer, a competent jockey is one who obtains the maximum level of performance the horse has to give, while avoiding a strategic mistake that prevents the horse from finishing as high as that level of performance would allow. To the casual observer, riding looks "easy" and such competence would seem a matter of course, but the exact opposite is true. Top jockeys are superb athletes whose sport is dangerous as well as physically and mentally demanding.

First, let's consider the physical qualifications. In addition to weighing under 110 or 112 pounds, jockeys must possess the strength and stamina to control a headstrong thousand-pound animal.

Simply maintaining the crouch required for the two minutes of racing requires such extraordinary leg strength that inexperienced riders find themselves unable to walk after dismounting. Sophisticated testing by physicians and psychologists has consistently found jockeys to be in the top 10 percent of all athletes.

While the rules of racing require that a jockey be aboard a horse when it crosses the finish line in order to be certified as the official winner of the race, they don't say he has to be breathing.

Back in 1953, jockey Frank Hayes was aboard a horse named Sweet Kiss at Belmont Park. From the start to the finish, the track announcer praised the exploits of jockey Hayes as he rode Sweet Kiss, a 20-1 shot, to victory. The applause turned to silence, however, when his lifeless body still atop the steed made him the first and, thus far, the only jockey to win a race while *dead*. An examination by a local physician (not a veterinarian) concluded that some time during the race, poor Frank had a heart attack and died.

But of all the quirks I have ever heard or read about over the years, the funniest occurred back on May 8, 1936. Jockey Ralph Neves was declared dead after a savage fall at Bay Meadows in San Francisco during the third race. His tearful wife sat motionless in the stands as many well-wishers were consoling her. But in true trooper form, the track management decided, "Racing must go on."

By the sixth race, his wife had been brought to the Jockeys' Room when suddenly pandemonium broke out as the alive Neves sprinted past the grandstand, half-dressed and still wearing his toe tag. "At one point," he said, "I think everyone on the damn track was chasing me." He fought his way through the crowd and burst into the Jockeys' Room, where his thoughtful and benevolent colleagues were passing the hat for his widow. She fainted at the sight of her newly resurrected husband, who stood in the doorway, demanding to be allowed to ride. He insisted that he didn't *feel* dead, but the stewards still refused to let him compete again that day. The following day, though, Ralphy boy got his revenge; he rode five winners and claimed the meet's top prize—a $500 watch donated by Bing Crosby.

Here are the leading jockeys at Finger Lakes for 2006 (trust me, they are all still alive):

Name	Starts	1st	2nd	3rd	Earnings
John R. Davila, Jr.	635	181	113	80	$2,028,320
Paul A. Nicol, Jr.	735	123	117	107	$1,579,842
Jeremias Flores	641	109	114	99	$1,345,360
Elaine Castillo	594	80	92	98	$949,852
Robert Messina	447	77	56	58	$950,227
Michael A. Davila, Jr.	634	74	78	110	$864,215
Jose David Osorio	426	70	64	54	$732,865
Omar Camejo	448	62	66	66	$789,328
Gabriel Suarez	461	55	66	67	$649,151

I have found that jockeys should be keyed in any pre-race analysis. Why, you ask? Because not only are they professional in their effort, they never give you a bad ride; and even if they don't finish where you think they should, there is a satisfaction that you learned something from the race.

First, let's begin with John Davila, Jr. At age forty-three, this native of Juncos, Puerto Rico, has been riding professionally for more than eighteen years. And while his first ride was in 1988 at Calder Race Course, he has progressed steadily since then, winning the 1995 Finger Lakes Budweiser Breeders' Cup aboard Not Surprising. Despite injuries, he owns four Finger Lakes riding titles ('94,'98,'02,'06); he has ridden the 2002 Finger Lakes Horse of the Year Runaway Tiger to all of her victories at "the Thumb," and he is a two-time winner of the New York Derby (1996: Carr Tech; 2003: Traffic Chief).

On a Tuesday, back in October 2006, John Davila, Jr., tied the record for most wins in one day at Finger Lakes Gaming and Racetrack. He now joins the multiple Finger Lakes jockeys who have accomplished the same feat.

The six-win day for Davila included four victories for leading trainer Chris Englehart. The horses saddled by Englehart that Davila won aboard were: Starship Wonder, which paid $6.80 to win;

Karakorum Ella ($3.10); Caught In the Zip ($5.40); and Karakorum Chance ($5.90). The six-time leading jockey also crossed the wire first with Sizzling Saint ($4.50) and Four Nine Whiskey ($7.20).

Davila came close to breaking the record in the ninth race when he finished second by three-quarters of a length aboard One El of a Lady. Incidentally, Robert Messina, who was in the saddle of the race winner, was the last jockey to win six on a card at Finger Lakes. Messina did it in 2001, when he also established a record for consecutive victories with seven. Kevin Whitley accomplished the feat in 1989 and 1992 and is another holder of the all-time record for most wins in one day at Finger Lakes. The list also includes John Grabowski (2000), Carlos Dominguez (1995), Leslie Hulet (1995), and Roger Cox (1971).

Next out of the gate is Joe Badamo, who is truly a hometown favorite. At age 42, this native of Seaford, New York, has been riding since 1986. Some of his accomplishments include being a seventh-leading rider at Aqueduct as an apprentice in 1987. From there, he secured his first career victory with 32-1 long-shot Winsome Bernard in the second race of his career; he won 16 of his first 50 and 26 of his first 100 career races. In 2003, he won the Arctic Queen Handicap aboard Ora. And today, he still holds a winning percentage of 22 for the past eight seasons combined.

By way of background, Badamo graduated from the Rochester Business Institute in 1994 with a 4.0 GPA in para-professional accounting. He's been known to run some strong numbers against his competition from mid-season through the fall.

The next jockey to be followed is Jeremias Flores. At age 31, the Canovanas, Puerto Rico, native rode his first mounts at El Commandante back in 1998. Later that year, he became leading apprentice rider at Finger Lakes and finished that season with 127 victories—fourth overall in the rider standings.

Next, there is the elder statesman of the quartet, Paul Nicol, Jr. At forty-five, this native of Annapolis, Maryland, has been riding for over 25 years. Nicol's first mounts came in 1981 with Parafool (MD). Some of his accomplishments include winning seven races on a nine-race card at Pimlico in June 1983; guiding Double Screen to victory in the 1997 Grade III Finger Lakes Breeders' Cup; owning the 1983 riding title at Pimlico; and in 1993, duplicating his title effort at Finger Lakes. I've seen this man at a mile-seventy break up easy superfectas with more moves than a four-way cold tablet.

In baseball, there was the adage of "Spahn and Sane and pray for rain." The same can be said of jockey John Davila, Jr., and trainer Chris Englehart at Finger Lakes. Another important paring is Charlton Baker and John Davilla.

	Champion Jockey	Wins	Champion Trainer	Wins
2005	John Davila, Jr.	153	Chris Englehart	118
2004	John Davila, Jr.	136	Chris Englehart	136
2003	John Davila, Jr.	138	Chris Englehart	95
2002	John Davila, Jr.	141	Michael S. Ferraro	85

While I have discussed both "seasoned" jockeys as well as "hot" jockeys, I think that apprentice jockeys have been given a bad rap for many years. Remember, every jockey in the Hall of Fame also was an apprentice.

By definition, an apprentice jockey offers a trainer one big advantage—weight allowance. In many races, particularly in the sprints (which make up a majority of the races), trainers have a keen eye towards them. The rule is—until the apprentice has five victories, he is given a ten-pound weight allowance in all races except handicap and stake races. From the time of the fifth victory through thirty more victories, the jockey is allowed a seven-pound allowance. In every race after the thirtieth win that occurs within a year from the date of the fifth win, the apprentice gets a five-pound allowance. Also, if an apprentice signs a contract with a stable, the apprentice gets a three-pound allowance for an additional year when riding that stable's horses.

True, they lack experience, but in lower-priced races, the rule of thumb is that these younger jockeys have a tendency to take the races more seriously and are willing to follow the orders of a trainer more diligently than a more experienced jockey.

A perfect example was Elaine Castillo, who during the 2003 and 2004 Finger Lakes racing seasons seemed like Hall of Famer Julie Krone. When I reviewed my sheets from that period, I found that in 68 percent of the races in which she was riding that I had bet in, she finished in the money 73 percent of the time.

In addition to knowing a track and knowing a trainer, there are instances when a "hot jockey" coming from an outside-post position can allow the speed of the race to let the competition run him into the ground.

Just like in other sports, there are given situations when a jockey can seem to do no wrong. Some say it's a time when the racing gods are trying to even the score. The superstitious believe that the winner of the first race often has an advantage going into the second, and if a given jockey was picked in the first, even without looking at the mount, the same jockey will be selected for the second race in the Daily Double.

Now let's look at item number four on the following page for the past performance data. Today, the *Daily Racing Form* lists some 39 separate pieces of information to aid you in analyzing a race:

1)	Exotic Wagers available for this race.
2)	Type of Race, Race Distance, Purse & Race Conditions.
3)	Track Program Number.
4)	Horse's color, sex, age, state where bred, sire, dam, and dam's sire.
5)	Owner.
6)	Quick line Numerical Assignments (CL-Class, PR-Probability, SP-Speed, PW-Probable Winner) reflecting the relative strength of each horse.
7)	Current Sire's Stud Fee rounded up to the nearest thousand.
8)	Weight horse carries with apprentice allowance.
9)	In to be claimed for.
10)	Today's jockey and mounts, wins, places, shows and win percentage for this year or if before April 1, this year and last year, Lifetime statistics including starts, wins, place, show and earnings.
12)	Morning Line.
13)	Trainer year statistics including starts, win, place, show and win percentage or if before Apr.1, this year and last year. Current Meet Statistics & Percentages.
14)	Statistical breakdown of last 2 years the horse raced with starts, wins, places, shows and money earned. For first three months of a given year, the top line will have earnings for that year plus the prior year (if horse raced in that prior year) and the line below will have earnings for the next most recent year the horse raced.
15)	Career turf record and earnings.
16)	Entry indicates horse is part of coupling PP indicates horse's postposition.
17)	Abbreviated Owners Colors.
18)	Record this track
19)	Career wet dirt record and earnings.
20)	Record this distance, today's surface.
21)	Date of last race, race number, track abbreviation, course, distance of race, track condition, fractions, final time, age restrictions, sex restriction, state restriction and class.
22)	Short line indicates a layoff of four months to a year; Long line indicates a layoff of more than a year.
23)	Type of race with purse in '000s for allowance, handicaps & non-graded stake.
24)	Lower case bold c indicates horse was claimed that race.
25)	Horse in bold type is entered in today's race.
26)	Number of horses that race.
27)	Latest Workout I Bullet Workout (fastest of day that track, that surface, that distance and horse's ranking of all horses who worked out that day at that distance of that surface.
28)	Ages that race.
29)	Average of Equibase Numbers.
30)	Horse's Equibase Number for that race.
31)	Points of Call and Finish.
32)	Jockey.
33)	Weight.
34)	B indicates that the horse wore blinkers; f indicates horse wore front bandages.
35)	Equiv. Odds — *Favorite.
36)	Average of Speed Ratings and Track Variants.
37)	Speed Rating and Track Variant.
38)	Winner of race and Weight.
39)	Short Comment.

After learning to read the past performances, the next logical step is the process of interpreting the information. One must remember that interpretation is nothing more or less than an expression of opinion rather than an irrefutable statement of fact. I would venture to say that if you put the same past performance sheet in front of ten handicappers, you'd probably get eleven different opinions.

Of all of this information supplied, however, here are the crucial things necessary for analyzing a race:

♣ SPEED

The speed rating listed in the form is usually a number assigned. It is made in comparison to the competition in a given race, not strictly in terms of just the clock. Over many years, however, I have learned that speed can also be the end to a great career. Take, for example, the career of a great racehorse named Count Fleet, who was owned by the wife of auto rental czar John Hertz.

Count Fleet, in his final four starts at age two and his first five starts at age three, was so far superior to his opposition that jockey John Longden put the horse away at the sixteenth pole and developed a reputation for "easing up" the horse. Many of Count Fleet's interior fractions in these races suggested a track or world record was on the way, but the jockey and trainer saw no reason to work the horse any harder than necessary for victory. As a result, many railbirds were left wondering just how fast Count Fleet could run if Longden wasn't always standing up as the horse approached the wire. But what was not apparent was the fact that owner Fannie Hertz had ordered it.

On one occasion, Hall of Fame sportswriter Red Smith asked Fannie why she wouldn't instruct trainer Cameron or jockey Longden to turn Count Fleet loose and go for the record. Her answer was simple, she said, "I thought that the object of the sport was to out-distance your opponents, not embarrass them!"

By the time the Belmont Stakes came around, Fannie, Longden, and Cameron all agreed that it was time to turn Count Fleet loose to see how fast he could run. But with only two weak opponents, going after a time record would be difficult. At post time, Count Fleet was five cents to the dollar, and the press corps, who had almost predetermined the finish before the race had even been run, gave Fannie a sick feeling.

In the race, much like that which the mighty Secretariat ran in the Belmont Stakes 30 years later, Count Fleet simply took off. By the time he reached the top of the stretch, Count Fleet was 20 lengths in front of the field. The margin reached 25 lengths at the wire. The colt missed the world record, but broke the Belmont Stakes record previously held by War Admiral in 1937.

To the applause of the crowd, Fannie, John, and Cameron headed for the winner circle. As was the practice, well-wishers and the press surrounded John as Fannie made a beeline to talk to the jockey and the groom. But amidst the archive pictures, Fannie showed a face painted with worry rather than either her stoic facade or partial smiles. Why? Because Count Fleet's racing career had come to an abrupt end. The ligament damage was so severe that Fannie decided he could never return to his prior form and that it was time to let the colt go to the breeding shed. As for speed, I'll always remember the words of Fannie Hertz, "I thought that the object of the sport was to outdistance your opponents, not embarrass them!"

♣ CLASS

The class rating is a combination of the breeding and pedigree of a given horse. The word is derived from the Greek word "klesis," which means "a calling or a summons." Since different kinds of summonses produce different responses, class eventually came to mean "a number of things grouped together because of certain likenesses or common traits," which is then compared to that of the competition. True, this is quite subjective, but in maiden races, you can often find a good trainer who wants to see if his owner's purchase is really worth the money.

Since one of the most reliable indications of the class of a race is the purse offered, the purses that a horse has earned are reflective of its class. Handicappers have developed several methods for comparing the earnings of horses to separate contenders from non-contenders.

The best indication of current class is the purse offered in each of the most recent races in which a horse raced well. This information is only available, however, by looking at past results charts (see pages 32–33).

Handicappers who must use past performances usually use one of three methods. The first is comparing total earnings for the year. Beautiful Contest, for example, earned $62,860 through November 5, 1979. By referring to a table earlier in this book, one can find that these earnings place Beautiful Contest in the top 1.5 percent of all horses that raced that year. These earnings may indicate that Beautiful Contest has demonstrated more class over the year than another horse that has raced approximately the same number of times, but comparing total earnings against those of more lightly raced horses in the same race can be very misleading.

To solve the problem of dealing with the relationship of races to earnings, many handicappers divide the number of races into total earnings to obtain each horse's average earnings per start. Beautiful Contest, for example, earned that $62,860 in 23 starts, for an average of $2,622 per start. To make the calculation easier, most people using this method drop the last three digits of the total earnings, dividing 62 by 23 to get a "rating" of 2.7. While some computer studies have shown that this is a useful way to identify contenders in certain kinds of races, average earnings per start are misleading for horses that have been racing without winning in tougher company than today's race. For example, a horse that has been finishing third or fourth in stake races may have a lower average earning per start than an animal winning lower-class contests.

BEAUTIFUL CONTEST

Owner: Alton Stable $37,500   115

	ST.	1ST	2ND	3RD	AMT.
1979	23	4	7	1	$62,869
1978	30	11	1	1	5,249

DTE	RACE # TRK	COND	DIST	SPD RATING	SPD RATING	SPD RATING	TYPE	PSN	PSN	1ST PSN	2ND PSN	3RD PSN	PSN	JCKY	EQ WT	HORSE WT	OUTCOME	FINISH
05 NOV 79	2 AQU	FST	1-1/8	:48 4/5	1:13-2/5	1:51-1/5	CLM C-30000	8	7	7	7	7	7	PINCAY L. JR	B 119	GENERAL H.D. 112 / SAL'S DREAM 119 / FOLLOW THAT DREAM 117	OUTRUN	8
24 OCT 79	6 AQU	FST	1-1/8	:48	1:13-3/5	1:54-3/5	CLM 25000	5	6	5	1	1	1	PINCAY L. JR	B 119	BEAUTIFUL CONTEST 119 / WIMPFYBELL 110 / ROYAL DATE 115	DRIVING	8
15 OCT 79	3 BEL	GD	1-1/8	:49-2/5	1:15	1:53-3/5	CLM 35000	3	2	3	5	5	5	PINCAY L. JR	B 117	SAL'S DREAM 114 / GENERAL H.D. 110 / PULL A CUTIE 117	TIRED	6
30 SEP 79	2 BEL	SLY	1-1/8	:47-1/5	1:12-3/5	1:52—3/5	CLM 25000	1	2	1	1	1	1	PINCAY L. JR	B 117	BEAUTIFUL CONTEST 117 / HARRY J. 117 / DARING DO 115	DRIVING	6
17 SEP 79	3 BEL	FST	1	:46-4/5	1:12-1/5	1:37-2/5	CLM 30000	5	7	5	6	6	6	ASMUSSEN C.B.	B 117	BIRKHILL 117 / PROPERLY PERSON 119 / FUN HOUR 117	NO FACTOR	7
29 AUG 79	2 BEL	SLY	1-1/8	:46-4/5	1:12-1/5	1:50	CLM 35000	6	2	1	1	1	2	SAUMELL L.	B 117	PULL A CUTIE 117 / BEAUTIFUL CONTEST 117 / PROPERLY PERSON 113	GAMELY	6
12 AUG 79	3 SAR	MY	1-1/8	:49-1/5	1:14-1/5	1:53	CLM 35000	3	5	4	2	2	2	SAUMELL L.	B 117	BROADWAY BUCK 117 / BEAUTIFUL CONTEST 117 / POKIE JOE 117	DRIFTED	8
29 JUL 79	5 BEL	FST	7F	:23-3/5	:47-2/5	1:25	CLM 35000	7	1	4	6	6	5	HERNANDEZ R.	B 117	DAPPER ESCORT 117 / GENERAL H.D. 108 / TERM PAPER 119	NO EXCUSE	7
13 JUL 79	9 BEL	FST	7F	:23	:46	1:24-4/5	CLM 35000	4	7	5	4	4	2	HERNANDEZ R.	B 117	TERM PAPER 117 / BEAUTIFUL CONTEST 117 / BYE BY BLUS 112	WIDE, MISSED	10
04 JUL 79	1 BEL	FST	6F	:22-2/5	:45-2/5	1:11-2/5	CLM 50000	3	8	9	9	9	8	HERNANDEZ R.	B 117	SUBORDINATE 112 / THIRD OF JULY 117 / SILVER SCREEN 117	OUTRUN	10

AFFIRMED

Owner: Harbor View Farm   126

AMT. $809,280
801,541

	ST.	1ST	2ND	3RD
1979	7	5	1	1
1978	11	8	2	0

DTE	RACE # TRK	COND	DIST	SPD RATING	SPD RATING	SPD RATING	TYPE	PSN	PSN	PSN	PSN	PSN	PSN	JCKY	WT	HORSE WT	OUTCOME	FINISH
29 AUG 79	0 BEL	SLY	1	:45	1:09-2/5	1:34	ALLOW-ANCE	3	1	1	1	1	1	PINCAY L. JR	122	AFFIRMED 122 / ISLAND SULTAN 115 / PREFONTAINE 117	RIDDEN OUT	3
29 AUG 79	NO WAGERING. EXHIBITION RACE RUN BETWEEN 7TH AND 8TH RACES.																	
24 JUN 79	8 HOL	FST	1-1/4	:45-3/5	1:34-1/5	1:58-2/5	GOLD CUP H.	1	2	1	1	1	1	PINCAY L. JR	132	AFFIRMED 132 / SIRLAD 120 / TEXT 119	DRIVING	10
20 MAY 79	8 HOL	FST	1-1/16	:44-4/5	1:09-1/5	1:41-1/5	CALI-FOR-NIAN	2	1	1	1	1	1	PINCAY L. JR	130	AFFIRMED 130 / SYNCOPATE 114 / HARRY'S LOVE 117	DRIVING	8
04 MAR 79	8 SA	FSTt	1-1/4	:46-2/5	1:34-1/5	1:58-3/5	SANTA ANITA H.	3	2	2	1	1	1	PINCAY L. JR	128	AFFIRMED 128 / TILLER 127 / PAINTED WAGON 115	SPEED TO SPARE	8
04 FEB 79	8 SA	GD	1-1/4	:47	1:35-3/5	2:01	C.H. STRUB	8	2	3	1	1	1	PINCAY L. JR	126	AFFIRMED 126 / JOHNNY'S IMAGE 115 / QUIP 115	HANDILY	9
20 JAN 79	8 SA	GD	1-1/8	:45-3/5	1:09-3/5	1:48	SAN FER-NANDO	4	3	4	5	3	2	CAUTHEN S.	126	RADAR AHEAD 123 / AFFIRMED 126 / LITTLE REB 120	DRIFTED OUT	8
07 JAN 79	8 SA	FST	7F	:22-3/5	:45	1:21	MALIBU	2	1	3	3	3	3	CAUTHEN S.	126	LITTLE REB 120 / RADAR AHEAD 123 / AFFIRMED 126	HEMMED INTO STR.	5
14 OCT 78	8 BEL	SLY	1-1/2	:45-1/5	2:01-4/5	2:27-1/5	J.C. GOLD CUP	2	2	3	3	4	5	CAUTHEN S.	121	EXCELLER 126 / SEATTLE SLEW 126 / GREAT CONTRACTOR 126	SADDLE SLIPPED	6
16 SEP 78	8 BEL	FST	1-1/8	:47	1:10-1/5	1:45-4/5	MARL-BORO H.	1	2	2	2	2	2	CAUTHEN S.	124	SEATTLE SLEW 126 / AFFIRMED 124 / NASTY AND BOLD 119	NO EXCUSE	6
19 AUG 78	8 SAR	FST	1-1/8	:48	1:36-4/5	2:02	TRA-VERS	3	2	2	1	1	1	PINCAY L. JR	126	AFFIRMED 126 – DQ / ALYDAR 126 / NASTY AND BOLD 126	CAME OVER	4

To correct this problem, one handicapper has adopted a third means of comparing earnings. This somewhat complicated method uses the horse plus total earnings to arrive at an approximation of the average total purse races in which the horse earned money.

Computing the average total, I based it on the percentage of how each purse is distributed to each horse. In the albeit crudest method, one starts with the fact that an average of 60 percent of the purse in a race goes to the winner; an average of 20 percent goes to the second-place horse; and an average of 10 percent goes to the third-place horse. Converting to decimals, the handle then multiplies the number of wins the horse has achieved by .6, the number of seconds by .2, and the number of thirds by .1, dividing the sum of these multiplications into the total earnings, providing an approximation of the average purse.

This method does not, of course, take into consideration the exact percentage applicable at each track, nor does it account for prize money awarded for places below third place.

If you'd like to do the exercise and see an example of the fallacy of this logic, look back to 1977 and compare Alydar to Affirmed. Based upon that logic, you might have burned several dollars during their two-year-old campaign and even the start of their three-year-old race to the Triple Crown (see page 33).

♣ DISTANCE

Although, theoretically, the ideal Thoroughbred is bred to combine speed and endurance and can be victorious at distances from six furlongs to a mile and a half, realistically, most horses will win in a narrow range of distances.

The distance rating is how often this horse has run at this distance and at this price. In addition, if it is not noted, you should look to see if there is any competition in the race that he has met before. How did he do? When this is combined with changes in equipment, however, you should beware. Often a trainer tries different things in the pursuit of a victory, but in the case of an older horse, I hold to the adage "You can't teach an old dog new tricks."

Over the years, I have seen that speed is easier to breed. I think back to a fellow former banker turned trainer, Laz Barerra. Back in 1978 while Affirmed was on his way to becoming the last Triple Crown champion, I remember asking Barerra how he thought he could win the Belmont—a distance of a mile and a half—with a horse whose lineage showed nothing when going long. He said to me, "Sometimes you can be successful in training a horse to go a mile and a quarter. But the extra quarter of a mile required in the Belmont is dependent on the heart and head of the horse alone . . . the horse will tell us if he can do it."

♣ STYLE

The running style rating is a combination of the old adage about horses for courses and the question of whether a horse comes from off the pace or is better at being on the pace. It is important to know that this number can be affected by changes in equipment and/or jockey.

I can only say to you that I've been busted more times than a novice blackjack player when a jockey seems to have a brain cramp and he/she tries to change the pattern of a horse's racing style.

There is one additional category that you will not find in the past performances that I call the intangibles. These are plus or minus factors that are based upon observations that you have made either mentally or as written notes on a given horse. This is different from the "Short Comment" piece of information.

Intangible ratings is a list of items that may make you take a second look at a horse who you might have discarded in your initial analysis. Such was the case with a horse that I followed for three years. The horse was Missionary Monk.

If I had to prepare a profile on him, it would read: seven furlongs on a fast track in claiming races with a purse range of $15,000 to $25,000 and assigned post-position numbers ranging from #3 to #6. Missionary Monk was the poor man's Forego. Initially slow of foot from the gate, he would plow his way through the first four furlongs and then develop a strong turn of foot for the last two furlongs. At distances in excess of seven furlongs, he would seem to need an oxygen mask to finish the race. In distances below seven furlongs, he would be outrun and would seem to be saying to the field, "Hey wait for me!"

During his racing career, he had more owners and trainers than Liz Taylor has had husbands. And it seemed that after each claim, they would try to change either his style or to build up his endurance. They even tried shopping him around to different tracks—Aqueduct, Suffolk, Philadelphia, Finger Lakes, and Delaware; he had more travel miles than a secretary of state. But wherever he ran, it always came back to his profile of seven furlongs.

Another intangible is equipment changes. While it is generally known that blinkers are used to promote early speed in a horse that has a tendency to do more observing of the competition rather than attempting to pass it, there are instances when this change of equipment is just what the doctor ordered. Conversely, the elimination of blinkers on some horses in distance races allows them to relax in the early part of a race, thereby conserving energy for the finish.

How well a horse stands up under the strain depends to a great extent on the condition of the surface over which he/she races. The ideal racing surface gives enough to absorb some of the shock of impact, and is elastic enough to return most of the energy to help the horse spring forward.

Hard surfaces are the fastest surfaces because they offer the least resistance. Because they absorb little or none of the force of impact, however, they place a great deal more stress on the horse's tendons, bones, and joints. The effect is quite similar to the knee and ankle problems commonly suffered by people who jog on asphalt roads.

Racecourses that are too loose or too soft, on the other hand, absorb a lot of energy, but they don't have any "give." That means the horse has to supply much more muscle power and tires more easily. The effect is much like that which people face trying to run on the beach or in the mud.

Turf is the closest nature comes to providing the best racing surface. The grass helps absorb the shock of impact and the root structure holds the soil together to provide a "springiness" that returns much of the energy to the horse. The problem with the turf course is that the grass is quickly worn away and becomes slippery and easily torn in wet weather.

Dirt courses have been designed to provide safe racing in all kinds of weather while emulating as closely as possible the advantages of natural grass. The courses are built in three layers. The bottom layer is crushed stone or gravel, which provides drainage. Next comes a six- to eight-inch mixture, primarily clay, that provides firmness. On the top is an approximately three-inch layer of sand and loam that serves as the cushion.

The exact composition and depth of each layer results in wide variations in surface from track to track. Hollywood and Santa Anita, for example, have relatively hard surfaces that produce very fast times. Tracks in the east, such as Belmont Park and Churchill Downs, tend to be deeper, more tiring, and slower.

Another element of track construction that affects both speed and the wear and tear on horses is the degree of banking of turns. Banking helps relieve the strain on the horse's inside legs; it makes it easier to avoid drifting, and it allows the turns to be negotiated at a higher speed. Unfortunately, the more pronounced the banking of turns, the more difficult the course is to maintain. Rain and gravity cause the top cushion to move toward the rail; "tracks" form on the course and interfere with the running of races. Because the expense of maintaining the racetrack comes out of the track's pockets, many in track management have tended to subordinate the welfare of the horses to the maintenance savings that come from flatter tracks.

Inadequate maintenance is another reason why many tracks develop pronounced "track biases"; track biases have a profound effect on the running of races. At some tracks, the rail gets pounded hard as asphalt, giving horses with inside post-positions a big advantage. At other tracks, natural contours result in the rail becoming heavier and deeper. Horses with inside post-positions tire more quickly, which gives the advantage to outside posts. The best jockeys are quick to notice track biases that occur from meeting to meeting or from day to day, and they concentrate on putting their mounts on the ideal track.

There were two jockeys who used opposite tactics. The first was Antonio Grael, or as he was known in New York, "Grael the Rail," for his belief that no matter what the conditions were, the shortest distance to the finish line was up the rail. The second was Hall of Fame jockey Angel Cordero, who was known for either riding the crown of the track or skipping along in the track marks created by the tractor prior to the start of the race.

The newly proclaimed Polytrak surfaces appear to be on the lips of all the handicappers around the town. I still can't seem to find any form of consistency, however, that will allow me to look at tracks that use it.

With those facts in mind, I then reviewed the 10-race card of November 20, 2006, and eliminated five races. The eliminations were the first, second, fifth, eighth, and ninth. With that spread, I knew that there was no betting any pick threes, pick sixes, or Daily Doubles. But good money management tells you that you never force a bet to try and get ahead; never put yourself in a hole, or as the old adage goes, "scared money can't win." It's sort of like trying to date identical twins. They may look the same, but the end result is heartache and a headache.

♣ FINGER LAKES: NOVEMBER 20, 2006—RACE 3

CLAIMING - For Thoroughbred Three Year Old and Upward (NW2 Y+)/
Claiming Price: $4,000/Six Furlongs On The Dirt/Purse: $8,000.

PN	ENTRY	JOCKEY	WEIGHT	MED.
5	Sway of Passion	Davilla, Jr., John	124	L f
6	Imafavoritetrick	Nicol, Jr., Paul	119	L b
2	After Sams Jazz	Alvarado, Nazario	124	L f
1A	Rodeo Raheem	Davilla, Jr., Michael	120	L b
1	Adaptation	Baez, Jose	119	L b
3	Elway's Way	Forkhamer, Pauline	119	L b
7	Frank Headley	Suarez, Gabriel	119	L b

PN	ENTRY	SPEED	CLASS	DISTANCE	STYLE	INTANGIBLES	TOTAL
1A.	Rodeo Raheem	7	6	5	7		25
1	Adaptation	7	5	6	6		24
2	After Sams Jazz	8	9	10	3		36
3	Elway's Way	6	7	7	8		28
5	Sway of Passion	10	8	9	9		36
6	Imafavoritetrick	9	10	8	10		37
7	Frank Headley	5	4	4	5		18

PN	ENTRY	WIN	PLACE	SHOW
5	Sway of Passion	3.40	2.20	2.10
6	Imafavoritetrick		3.30	2.80
2	After Sams Jazz			3.90

EXACTA	8.20	TRIFECTA	48.20

So far, you have heard me talk about analyzing a race. The process of elimination consists of six components in terms of the field of horses. These are the speed, class, distance, running style, and intangibles. Listed below is the chart that I use for Finger Lakes.

	5 furlongs	6 furlongs	7 furlongs	1 mile 70yds.
Speed	8	7	5	5
Class	4	4	5	6
Distance	6	6	7	7
Running style	6	6	7	7
Track condition	6	6	7	8
Intangibles	10	7	8	8
Total	36	36	39	41

♣ FINGER LAKES: NOVEMBER 20, 2006—RACE 4

CLAIMING - For Thoroughbred Three Year Old and Upward/Fillies and Mares (NWI 6M)/Claiming Price: $4,000/Six Furlongs On The Dirt/Purse: $8,000.

PN	ENTRY	JOCKEY	WEIGHT	MED.
8	Prospectforme	Alvarado, Nazano	124	L bf
6	Shining Forever	Nicol, Jr., Paul	124	L b
1	Winloc Majesty	Suarez, Gabriel	124	L bf
7.	Diamondsfora Lady	Castillo, Elaine	124	L bf
4	Wee Geht's	Davilla, Jr., Michael	124	L b
3	Royal Speech	Ignacio, Rodolfo	124	L b
1A	Panina	Rivera, David	124	L b
2	Watrals Bashfull	Morales, Daniel	124	L

PN	ENTRY	SPEED	CLASS	DISTANCE	STYLE	INTANGIBLES	TOTAL
1	Winloc Majesty	8	8	10	9		35
1A	Panina	7	7	10	8		32
2	Watrals Bashfull	6	6	7	7		26
3	Royal Speech	4	4	6	5		19
4	Wee Geht's	5	5	5	6		26
6	Shining Forever	10	9	8	8		25
7	Diamondsfora Lady	3	3	4	4		14
8	Prospectforme	9	10	9	10		38

PN	ENTRY	WIN	PLACE	SHOW
8	Prospectforme	8.80	4.10	2.40
6	Shining Forever		3.90	2.20
1	Winloc's Majesty			2.10

EXACTA	34.00	TRIFECTA	62.00

♣ FINGER LAKES: NOVEMBER 20, 2006—RACE 6

MAIDEN -1 Mile and Seventy Yards/For Maidens, Fillies Two-Year-Olds/
Purse: $17,000.

PN	ENTRY	JOCKEY	WEIGHT	MED
5	Hi	Davilla, Jr., John	120	
8	Old Hussy	Ruis, Luis	120	L
1	Santa Fe Babe	Nicol, Jr., Paul	120	L
2	Oxford Girl	Sone, Joel	120	L
3	CasuilHint	Floras, Jose	120	L
4	Knownowthisistrue	Rideout, Roberto	113	L b
6	Beforthewestwaswon	Osorio, David	120	
7	SceneNHeard	Castillo, Elaine	120	L
9	So Gracious	Alvarado, Noberto	120	L

PN	ENTRY	SPEED	CLASS	DISTANCE	STYLE	INTANGIBLES	TOTAL
1	Santa Fe Babe	10	10	9	8		37
2	Oxford Girl	5	3	5	7		20
3	CasuilHint	6	4	4	5		19
4	Knownowthisistrue	7	6	6	6		25
6	Beforthewestwaswon	8	5	5	4		22
7	SceneNHeard	9	9	10	10		38
8	Old Hussy	8	8	8	9		33
9	So Gracious	8	7	7	5		27

PN	ENTRY	WIN	PLACE	SHOW
1	Santa Fe Babe	8.50	5.30	3.70
7	SceneNHeard		4.90	3.70
9	So Gracious			7.80

EXACTA	42.80	TRIFECTA	326.50

As you can see from my analysis, the three horses that I favored were Santa Fe Babe, So Gracious, and Scene N Heard.

Now let's look at the same track on a day where I had made my selections the night before, only to see a storm come in that night and leave me to re-analyze my choices because I had to deal with track conditions classified as "sloppy," which then changed to "muddy" on race day just prior to the first race.

Even well maintained racing strips differ substantially from day to day due to the weather. Differences in drainage and drying can make one part of the track faster than another. The following general track conditions are posted for the racing public:

Fast
Usually means that the cushion is dry and the base is firm. "Dry," however, can vary from dusty to moist enough to press into clods, and the range caused by these differences can mean as much as a two- or three-second variation in time over six furlongs. Many horses dislike the footing that results when clods form under their hooves. This condition is referred to as a "cuppy" track.

Sloppy
Usually means that the track surface is covered with puddles, but the base is firm. Sloppy tracks are generally about as speedy as "fast" tracks, but because some come-from-behind horses dislike having slop splashed back in their faces, such tracks tend to favor speed horses.

Muddy
Tracks are labeled muddy when water has had a chance to seep into the track's base, making it soft. The softer or "heavier" the track, the greater the effect on horses that tend to tire more easily.

Good
This term is most commonly used to describe a drying track that's progressing from muddy to fast; it is sometimes used to describe a track moving from fast to sloppy. Conditions within the label "good" vary widely, depending on exactly how much moisture has been absorbed by the cushion and the base.

Slow
Is a rather archaic term seldom used today; this description applies to a track between muddy and good.

Heavy
Also rarely used today; this word describes a track that's worse than muddy, in which the base has become gooey rather than soft as a result of a long stretch of wet weather.

Sometimes the performance of a horse improves dramatically on what is often called an "off" track, while the performance of others drops off sharply. Also, while many prefer a speed horse on a sloppy track because they escape the mud being thrown in their faces, others prefer come-from-behind horses on tiring, muddy tracks.

Such was the case back on November 13, 2006; the track looked more like a drying swamp than a racetrack. After three separate times looking at the race card, I decided to bet on five races: 1-2-3-4-6

♣ FINGER LAKES: NOVEMBER 13, 2006—RACE 1

CLAIMING - For Three Year Olds and Upward/Claiming Price: $4,000/
One Mile and Seventy Yards/Purse: $8,500.

PN	ENTRY	JOCKEY	WEIGHT	MED
1	WolfEye	Cabassas, Anton	124	L
1A	Setters Beach	Buckley, Johnathan	124	L
2	Damthefrost	Dominguez, Callos	124	L
3	Joe's Command	Davilla, Jr., Michael	124	L
4	Monetary Dancer	Osorio, David	124	L
6	He's So Handsome	Flores, Jose	124	L

PN	ENTRY	SPEED	CLASS	DISTANCE	STYLE	INTANGIBLES	TOTAL
1	WolfEye	10	9	9	10		38
1A	Setters Beach	10	9	8	9		36
2	Damthefrost	7	7	7	7		28
3	Joe's Command	8	6	6	6		26
4	Monetary Dancer	9	7	5	7		24
6	He's So Handsome	6	4	4	4		18

PN	ENTRY	WIN	PLACE	SHOW
1	WolfEye	3.10	2.90	2.20
1A	Settlers Beach	3.10	2.90	2.20
4	Monetary Dancer			2.60

EXACTA	8.80

The first race had a six-horse field going one mile and seventy yards. The race boiled down to the fact that trainer Tom Agosti had an entry of WolfEye and Settlers Beach which, on paper, appeared to be miles ahead of the rest of the field. The second horse in the race that I looked at was Vandiano, but he had been scratched before and the odds of him producing a decent exacta were slim to none; even if he beat the entry, the most that it would pay would be $12 to $15. The third horse of choice could be Monetary Dancer. But the answer was still the same—a payment of 12-15. Against my better judgment, I made a six-dollar bet. Normally, you don't play for an even-money return, but I decided to break my own rule.

The race result was WolfEye and Settlers Beach followed by Monetary Dancer; Vandiano was scratched, and the exacta paid $8.80, and, yes, I lost money. But I learned one thing from the race—jockey Cabassas was on his game for the day. I've seen him when he gets on a run, taking the equivalent of a plow horse to victory.

♣ FINGER LAKES: NOVEMBER 13, 2006—RACE 2

CLAIMING - For Fillies and Mares-Three Year Olds and Upward which have never won four races/Claiming Price: $4,000/One Mile and Seventy Yards/Purse: $8,500.

PN	ENTRY	JOCKEY	WEIGHT	MED
1	Darby Book	Flores, Jose	120	L
2	Forever Flawless	Forkhamer, Pauline	120	L
3	Make Fast	Davilla, Jr., John	122	L
4	Heated Expression	Baez, Jose	117	L
5	Landing Gear	Nicol, Jr., Paul	120	L
6	Miss Bernadette	Buckley, Johnathan	122	L
7	Jet To Rome	Morales, David	120	L
8	Golden Goddess	Davilla, Jr., Michael	120	L

PN	ENTRY	SPEED	CLASS	DISTANCE	STYLE	INTANGIBLES	TOTAL
1	Darby Book	3	4	4	5		16
2	Forever Flawless	7	2	4	4	2	19
3	Make Fast	6	6	8	8	7	35
4	Heated Expression	5	7	5	6	4	217
5	Landing Gear	5	6	4	5		20
6	Miss Bannerette	6	9	7	7	7	36
7	Jet To Rome	4	5	6	5	5	25
8	Golden Goddess	7	6	8	6		27

PN	ENTRY	WIN	PLACE	SHOW
6	Miss Bannerette			
8	Golden Goddess			
4	Heated Expression			

EXACTA	31.20	TRIFECTA	84.00

The second race I also passed up. It appeared to be a duplicate of the first in distance and purse, but the caliber was slower. At first glance, it looked as though the competition would have a hard time finishing the mile and seventy yards in under 1:50.0. To my way of thinking, that's hourglass time, and with a field of eight, I could only eliminate three horses. So while the payoff might be good, the bet on both an exacta box and a trifecta box seemed too risky. I decided to make a $6 mind bet on Miss Bannerette, Make Fast, and Landing Gear, eliminating Golden Goddess and Heated Expression in an exacta.

Surprise! The race result proved me wrong. The order of finish was Miss Bannerette, Golden Goddess, and Heated Expression, with the exacta paying $31.20 and the trifecta paying $84.00.

But I did again learn something that I needed to put in my memory bank—Golden Goddess was not a morning glory, and the workout numbers were for real.

♣ FINGER LAKES: NOVEMBER 13, 2006—RACE 3

MAIDEN - For foaled New York State and approved by the New York State-Bred Registry Maidens, Three-Year-Olds and Upward/Five and One Half Furlongs/ Purse: $19,500.

PN	ENTRY	JOCKEY	WEIGHT	MED
1	Regal Encounter	Buckley, Paul	121	L
2	ManhassetBayCat	Forkhammer, Pauline	121	
3	Sea Lore	Suarez, Gabriel	124	L
4	Castleman	Messina, Robert	121	L
5	Louiethelocksmith	Rivera, David	121	L
6	Oughta Be a Jet	Castillo, Elaine	121	L
7	Remote View	Morales, David	121	L
8	Spytex	Camejo, Omar	121	
9	RedArt	Flores, Jose	124	L

PN	ENTRY	SPEED	CLASS	DISTANCE	STYLE	INTANGIBLES	TOTAL
1	Regal Encounter	7	7	7	7		28
2	ManhassetBayCat	6	6	6	10		28
3	Sea Lore	9	9	10	9		37
4	Castleman	10	10	9	9	+2	40
5	Louiethelocksmith	5	5	5	8		23
6	Oughta Be a Jet	4	4	4	6		18
7	Remote View	3	3	3	5		14
8	Spytex	2	6	6	6		20
9	RedArt	8	8	8	8	+2	38

PN	ENTRY	WIN	PLACE	SHOW
4	Castleman	7.10	2.90	2.60
9	RedArt		2.30	2.10
3	Sea Lore			2.80

EXACTA	18.40	TRIFECTA	59.50

The third race was a 5½-furlong sprint for maiden special weights. Normally, I eliminate post-positions 8 through 12 in sprints of that short a distance because of the track circumference, particularly at Finger Lakes. It is very rare that a young horse has enough speed to break from that far outside without losing stamina. It's a race that inside speed rules. But there is a possibility when the horse in question has a significantly higher speed rating over the competition to finish in the top three.

First, let's look at the eliminations. Regardless of track conditions, Darby Book lacked in four categories: speed, class, distance, and style. Jockey Flores didn't seem to appear with a cape and a big S on his chest either. The same can be said of Forever Flawless and Jet to Rome; plus both had an aversion to running well in the mud.

With the late scratch of Darby Book, I was down to five possibilities (3-4-5-6-8). Now left with five; the track conditions eliminated both Make Fast and Landing Gear, leaving us with Heated Expression, Miss Bannerette, and Golden Goddess (4-6-8). While I still had a queasy feeling about eliminating Make Fast with Davilla aboard, his intangibles ranked lower in that race than that of the other three entrants.

While I hit both the exacta and the trifecta based upon what I saw and analyzed, late-money bets dropped the odds to a payout of $18.40 for the exacta and $59.50 for the trifecta. On one hand, I made $38.95 on a $12 bet—remember, all of my bets are in $1.00 increments—which is better than losing, but the lesson learned is that late money always reads the racing form and little money is always better than no money at all. In addition, I would be betting the next race with house money and not mine.

♣ FINGER LAKES: NOVEMBER 13, 2006—RACE 4

CLAIMING - For Thoroughbred Three Year Old and Upward (NW2 6M)/
Claiming Price: $4,000/Five and One Half Furlongs On The Dirt/Purse: $8,000.

PN	ENTRY	JOCKEY	WEIGHT	MED
6	Dancingontheceiling	Cabassa, Jr., Abad	120	L
7	Passing Ships	Nicol, Jr., Paul	120	L b
9	Aeras	Davilla, Jr., John	124	L bf
8	The Queen's Doc	Davilla, Jr., Michael	120	L b
5	Kiss an Optimist	Messina, Robert	122	L b
1	No I Can't	Camejo, Omar	122	L
3	Alaki's Jet	Sone, Joel	122	L f
2	Lord Buckley	Flores, Jeremias	120	L
4	Alyfriend	Morales, Daniel	120	L bf

PN	ENTRY	SPEED	CLASS	DISTANCE	STYLE	INTANGIBLES	TOTAL
6	Dancingontheceiling	10	8	9	10		37
7	Passing Ships	9	9	10	9		37
9	Aeras	8	10	8	8		34
8	The Queen's Doc	7	7	7	7		28
5	Kiss an Optimist	6	5	5	6		22
2	Lord Buckley	5	6	6	5		22
4	Alyfriend	5	6	6	5		22
3	Alaki's Jet	4	4	4	5		17
1	No I Can't	5	4	5	4		18

PN	ENTRY	WIN	PLACE	SHOW
6	Dancinontheceihng	12.00	6.00	4.00
7	Passing Ships		4.40	3.70
9	Aeras			4.00

EXACTA	52.00	TRIFECTA	292.00

What I also knew was that Dancingontheceiling previously had been running in $6,000 claiming races at Fort Erie in Canada and $3,500 claiming races at Suffolk Downs in Boston at the same distance. Trainer Poliziani seemed to be following his typical form of looking for a track and a price. In this case, after running at both of those tracks, he sent the horse to Finger Lakes for a $4,000 claiming race; the horse was not changing his class competition. If the track condition hadn't been muddy, however, I would have only bet the 6-7 exacta for a $35.00 return.

Such was the case when I boxed a 6-7-9 $1 exacta and a $1 tri-fecta after having downgraded all the front-end speed and watched a "hot jockey" come from off the pace to win. Note that all the speed finished fourth, fifth, and sixth.

As you can see, a $12 bet returned $172.00 ($6 box exacta and $6 box trifecta) or 14.33 times my initial investment.

Going into the 6th race, I was ahead $230.95, having only spent $24.00 of my original $40.00 on two races.

Now let's look at the analysis of the sixth race.

♣ FINGER LAKES, NOVEMBER 13, 2006—RACE 6

MAIDEN SPECIAL WEIGHT - For Thoroughbred Two-Year-Old Fillies
One Mile And Seventy Yards On The Dirt/Purse: $17,000.

PN	ENTRY	JOCKEY	WEIGHT	MED
2	Santa Fe Babe	Nicol, Jr, Paul	120	L
7	Scene N Heard	Castillo, Elaine	120	L
8	So Gracious	Cabassa, Jr., Abad	120	L b
1A	Old Hussy - DQ	Rodriguez, Pedro	120	L b
1	Highwaytohappiness	Davilla Jr., John	120	
6	Beforthewestwaswon	Osono, Jose	120	f
3	Oxford Girl	Sone, Joel	120	L b
5	Knownowthisistrue	Rideout, Ronny	116	L b
4	Casual Hint	Flores, Jeremias	120	L b

PN	ENTRY	SPEED	CLASS	DISTANCE	STYLE	INTANGIBLES	TOTAL
2	SantaFeBabe	10	10	10	10	+1	41
3	Oxford Girl	7	7	7	7		28
4	Casual	5	6	6	8		25
5	Knownowthisistrue	6	6	10	7		29
1	Highwaytohappiness	9	8	8	9		34
6	Beforthewestwaswon	8	9	8	8		37
7	Scene N Heard	9	9	9	9		40
1A	Old Hussy	8	8	8	9	+4	37
8	So Gracious	7	7	10	10	+7 jockey change	41

PN	ENTRY	WIN	PLACE	SHOW
2	Santa Fe Babe	8.50	5.30	3.70
7	Scene N Heard		4.90	3.70
8	So Gracious			7.80

EXACTA	42.80	TRIFECTA	326.50

Now I had my chance to see if Cabassas was real or Memorex. He was aboard a horse named So Gracious. On paper, he looked like an also ran, but the intangible of Cabassas was that he had been riding through the mud all day like a duck cruising on the water of a placid pond. So I figured him in my box. The shoot-out for first and second would be between the remaining favorites Santa Fe Babe and Scene N Heard. While the public had looked at Flores on Casual Hint, Flores appeared to be in pain after his dismount from the prior race. On his way back to the jockey's room, he had a decided limp. The limp was still there as he came to the paddock for this race. Although I could see the official asking him something, I knew that he was lying and that he was hurt. That was all I needed to put him and his mount in the also-ran pile. Remember what I said earlier about athletes in general and jockeys in particular: they lie about injuries. The investment for the race was 2-7-8 exacta and trifecta boxed.

♣ FINGER LAKES, NOVEMBER 20, 2006—RACE 7

Maiden Special Weight for two-year-olds going 5 _ furlongs.

PN	ENTRY	JOCKEY	WEIGHT	MED.
7	Head Stream	Davilla, Jr., Michael	120	
4	Radio Gem	Osorio, Jose	120	
6	Waracha	Alvarado, Nazarro	120	L f
5	Glorious Glory	Messina, Robert	122	b
2B	Rocket Run	Flores, Jeremias	120	L b
1A	Marcy Avenue	Baze, Jose	120	L b
3	Ink A Dink A Dink	Nicol, Jr., Paul	120	
2	Coeur de Or	Sone, Joel	120	L

PN	ENTRY	SPEED	CLASS	DISTANCE	STYLE	INTANGIBLES	TOTAL
1A	Marcy Avenue	6	6	6	6	+1	25
2	Coeur de Or	7	7	7	7		28
2B	Rocket Run	7	7	7	7		28
3	Ink A Dink A Dink	7	8	6	5		26
4	Radio Gem	9	9	9	9	+4	40
5	Glorious Glory	8	9	9	8	+3	37
6	Waracha	10	9	8	8	+5	40
7	Head Stream	9	8	9	9	+6	41

PN	ENTRY	WIN	PLACE	SHOW
7	Head Stream	17.80	9.90	5.60
4	Radio Gem		15.20	6.90
6	Waracha			2.70

EXACTA	368.50	TRIFECTA	1,325.00

As I looked at the form, the morning odds showed that **Coeur de Or** appeared to be the favorite, but all I saw from looking at the horse in the paddock area was a tired, head-sunken horse. Nor could I see jockey Joel Sone taking this horse and putting him on the lead or, at least, up on the pace. The next horse that I eliminated was **Rocket Run**, because I didn't believe that Flores was well enough to make this horse relax when the pressure started to come at him.

Normally, I don't like a horse with outside posts in 5½-furlong races, but with the speed that Headstream had showed he was definitely in the mix. So from the start, I looked at a fresh **Headstream** with Michael Davilla aboard pushing the pace and the battle for second between Radio Gem and Waracha.

♣ FINGER LAKES, NOVEMBER 20, 2006—RACE 8

CLAIMING – For Three Year Olds And Upward (NW4 L)/Claiming Price: $10,000 - $8,000/Five and One Half Furlongs/On The Dirt/Purse: $9,500.

PN	ENTRY	JOCKEY	WEIGHT	MED.
7	Shachner	Gutierrez, Jose	122	L bf
4	Cheetah Speed	Messina, Robert	122	L bf
6	Successful Secrets	Nicol, Jr., Paul	117	L b
5	Tale of Wonder	Flores, Jeremias	120	L f
8	Philly Frenzy	Badamo, Joseph	113	L bf
3	Prowling Wolf	Morales, Daniel	122	L bf
1A	Sweet Lucy Grace	Osorio, Jose	120	L
2.	No Crying Allowed	Baze, Jose	116	L b

PN	ENTRY	SPEED	CLASS	DISTANCE	STYLE	INTANGIBLES	TOTAL
1A	Sweet Lucy Grace	10	8	8	8	+7	41
2.	No Crying Allowed	3	3	7	9		22
3.	Prowling Wolf	4	5	6	7		22
4.	Cheetah Speed	9	9	9	9		36
5.	Tale of Wonder	5	6	5	8		24
6.	Successful Secrets	6	7	10	10	+4	37
7.	Shachner	10	10	9	9	+2	40
8.	Philly Frenzy	2	4	4	4		14

PN	ENTRY	WIN	PLACE	SHOW
7	Shachner	7.60	4.70	3.80
4	Cheetah Speed		3.30	3.30
6	Successful Secrets			4.20

EXACTA	29.20	TRIFECTA	97.50

By this point, the play of the day was to get to the fourth lane path, which seemed like the express lane all day. From the analysis, it looked like a four-horse race in the mud: Shachner, Successful Secrets, Cheetah Speed, and Tale of Wonder. And with all the speed tending to be on the outside, the determination was first to eliminate and then to look into the paddock area for any signals that might downgrade the selections. Since there was nothing new and Flores still looked hurt, I confirmed my belief that he could be eliminated, so the investment was 4-6-7 box exacta and trifecta.

When I think about off-track runners, my mind goes back to a horse aptly named Thunder Puddles. Even in a monsoon, he looked as comfortable as Gene Kelly did dancing in the movie "Singing in the Rain."

Since I have now exceeded my target return, the remaining races are simply mind bets. I have said it before—I have learned that there is no such thing as a streak: either you analyzed the race correctly or not. Too often I have seen people who don't walk away happy, but end up leaving with a "should-da, could-da quit" look.

CHAPTER THREE

Great Lakes Downs

OF ALL THE tracks that i have followed closely for the past seven years, Great Lakes Downs has been the most perplexing. It's similar to the cliché "The road to hell is paved with good intentions."

For those of you not familiar with Michigan, the town of Muskegon is situated in the western portion of the state, near the shores of Lake Michigan. Great Lakes Downs is near Muskegon Airport. The track commenced its first Thoroughbred meet on April 23, 1999. The facility has a five-furlong oval and was previously used as a Standardbred harness track. Great Lakes replaced the Detroit Race Course (DRC) on the Michigan-racing schedule after a tenure that spanned 49 years. DRC closed its doors at the end of the 1998 season. In the days of DRC, the major race was the Frontier Handicap. It has had a history that dates back over three decades; Ace Commander won three consecutive renewals of the race from 1974–76; Badwagon Harry, the 1984 Frontier winner, was also victorious in the 1985 running of the Michigan Mile and the State's only graded race—One-Eighth Handicap. Michigan Mile, as the race is commonly known, might be revived in future seasons.

Back then the track became the second home of the auto plant assembly line workers and families that didn't go to the ball game at

Detroit Stadium. It was also the home of the cheap date for couples attending summer school at the University of Michigan.

In February 2000, Magna Entertainment (MEC) acquired Great Lakes Downs and, despite the loss of DRC, Great Lakes committed to offer 22 stake races during the season, with each of them carrying a $50,000 guaranteed purse. On August 25, 2004, after four years of increasing losses, Magna announced in a press release that they were leasing the facility to Richmond Racing.

Early in January 2007, it appeared that the other shoe was about to drop when track General Manager Amy MacNeil spoke to the *Muskegon Chronicle* and was quoted saying, "We're not going to throw in the towel . . . our goal is to have a hugely successful season and give the horsemen a reason to come back." But the fact still remains that the parent company, Magna Entertainment, who owns or operates some 11 tracks across America and one in Vienna, said that they had lost about $1.8 million during 2006. They stated that "without significant changes in the regulatory environment that restricts horse racing from competing on a level playing field with other forms of gaming and entertainment, MEC had been unable to make Great Lakes profitable." MEC further implied that if the ever-increasing unemployment rate in Michigan didn't change, they may well be thinking of bailing out. Sad to say, but it appeared that Great Lakes would not secure some form of major assistance from the State and that the 2007 racing season (which runs from May through early November) would be its last.

At this point, I think it's only fair that for journalistic integrity I make mention of the fact that like other sports or, in fact, any business where money is concerned, there are elements that find it more palatable to try to beat the system and inflict their form of "get rich quick" chicanery rather than play by the rules.

In the December 20, 2006, edition of the *Daily Racing Form*, writer Matt Hegarty wrote, "The racing-industry investigation that led to the Tuesday bans of seven jockeys at Tampa Bay Downs traces in part to at least one race run at Great Lakes Downs in Michigan late this past summer, according to several racing officials with knowledge of the investigation."

Hegarty continued, "The race was targeted by investigators after bettors at Delaware Park cashed a large number of suspicious wagers on the race, according to the officials. One of the riders banned on Tuesday by Tampa Bay, Terry Houghton, rode in the race in question, the officials said."

Hegarty went on to say, "Herberto Rivera, a former steward at Great Lakes Downs, who is now a regional representative of the Jockeys' Guild, said that when Great Lakes ended its racing season on November 7th, the investigation into the race was still considered 'open.' Rivera also said that investigators from the Thoroughbred Racing Protective Bureau at Tampa Bay questioned the jockeys who were banned last week about the Great Lakes race."

Hegarty continued on: "I'm assuming it's the same race they're looking into because the TRPB took it over from us," said Rivera, who was a steward during the 2006 Great Lakes meet. Rivera said he could not comment on why the race was under investigation.

Two racing officials who had knowledge of the investigation confirmed that the Tampa ban was related to the investigation at Great Lakes Downs and Delaware Park. The officials said they could not be identified because the investigation is still ongoing. One of the officials said that another race at Great Lakes involving Houghton was also being investigated.

None of the officials would disclose or could identify the race or races in question.

Although Rivera said that investigators did not uncover anything suspicious about Houghton's rides, he implied that several aspects of the case had not been answered by the time the meet ended.

Three of the jockeys banned by Tampa—Houghton, Jose Delgado, and Joseph Judice—were among the top 20 leading riders at Great Lakes this year. Houghton led the standings by a wide margin, with 185 wins from 724 mounts.

But there is one thing that I have seen when it comes to investigations concerning the "Sport of Kings"—after an accusation is presented, the parties are guilty until proven innocent. Initially, it makes no difference whether or not the charges are a "bum rap." Because the penalty structure is so unevenly distributed by the "Lords of the Livery," the concept of "innocent until proven guilty" runs a distant second to press leaks filled with supposition purported primarily by undisclosed sources.

Even if it is eventually proven that the jockeys in this case are guilty of fixing races and they should have the book thrown at them, the punishment is meted out at opposite ends of the spectrum. It's either life or the equivalent of a house arrest.

What makes the matter even worse is the disparity of handling jockeys versus trainers. Is it fair to deny jockeys an opportunity to make a living until the matter has been adjudicated? There are plenty of trainers that have been accused of "juicing" horses. They don't get suspended or ruled off the grounds until a positive test is obtained. Why is it different for the riders? Why is the racing game so inconsistent? These jocks can't compete at some tracks, but are allowed to ride at others. The rules have to be consistent, or the general public will always view the game with a narrow eye. Why do the medication rules differ from jurisdiction to jurisdiction? Why are the disqualification and wagering rules different from state to state? The way this investigation is going, if the powers that be in the racing industry fail to find criminal behavior, then the lawsuits should be astronomical.

The question also becomes, how honest is racing?

Racing crimes generally fall into two classes—off-track and on-track. Those members of the computer generation remember the 2002 Breeders' Cup superfecta heist, where computer analyst Glen DeSilva and his two frat brother friends, Dereck Davis and Chris Harn, tried to commit wire fraud by creating a fictitious Pic 6 winning ticket on the October 26th Breeders' Cup through the Empire State Off-Track Betting Parlor.

Recent race-fixing trials and accusations of misdoing have unfortunately resulted in very misleading impressions of the integrity of the sport of Thoroughbred racing. Part of this impression results from the dishonesty that marred the early days of racing in both Britain and the United States. The truth is that, in this century, the combined efforts of state governments, the Jockey Club, and local racing associations have made Thoroughbred racing one of the best supervised and best policed of all professional sports. Every racetrack employee, no matter how lowly, is thoroughly investigated in a licensing procedure. Racetracks conduct elaborate pre- and post-race drug testing; they also employ increasingly sophisticated horse identification procedures. The Thoroughbred Racing Protective Bureau, whose investigators are primarily well trained ex-FBI agents, provides exhaustive surveillance of track activities. State as well as track auditors scrutinize computer printouts of wagering data to detect unusual patterns. Because of such scrutiny, the racing industry has a better record of deterring fraud than most corporations.

This does not mean, however, that certain individuals don't attempt to increase their income by misleading the public. Given the low purses at many tracks, trainers and jockeys sometimes have to rely on betting to make ends meet. Trainers try to push up odds on a horse by entering it in unsuitable races with unfit conditions, or by instructing the jockey to "hold" the horse. A few trainers even try to ensure success by injecting the horse with some new miracle drug. Fortunately, those trainers who aren't caught seldom succeed in the long run. Horsemen involved in shady practices are rarely competent enough at their profession to train their animals to the peak of fitness necessary to win after the odds have been built up. Although drugs can alleviate painful physical ailments, there's no evidence that they can overcome the limitations of a horse's natural ability. That true ability is usually reflected somewhere in the horse's past performances.

More serious than the isolated maneuvering of trainers and jockeys are betting coups or fixed races. The legalization of off-track betting and the increasing volume of betting on football, basketball, and baseball, however, have reduced dramatically the volume of illegal betting on horse races. Bookies will take small wagers on races, but they won't accept large bets because they don't get enough action to justify the risk involved.

To fix a race to ensure that one horse will win, or that certain horses will finish first and second, a prospective fixer would have to pay off several jockeys—a risky proposition. More importantly, to make up the cost of the bribes, the fixer would then have to bet a large amount to win. That large amount, in the pari-mutuel system, would depress odds to the unprofitable level.

Thus, attempts to fix races by on-track personnel are almost exclusively limited to trifecta, superfecta, pick 3, 4, and 6 races. But, since the probability of eliminating exotic wagers—thereby eliminating the incentive to cheat—are about as acceptable an option to the track as a poor man running for public office, the betting public, therefore, has to believe that both the on-track and off-track personnel continue to expand and improve the controls on exotic wager races so that the race-goer can bet with the level of confidence with which he bets in casinos or on other professional sports.

In addition to constantly improving the controls, I think that it's easy for a jockey to "hold" a horse, but it's impossible to bribe a jockey to ensure that his horse will win. Even if one race could be "fixed," thousands of combinations of horses would have to be played in the other races in order to guarantee picking the six winners.

♣ THE LEADING TRAINERS FOR 2006

Name	Starts	1st	2nd	3rd	Win %	$ %	Purses
Gerald S. Bennett	430	98	68	62	23	53	$1,052,966
Robert M. Gorham	374	76	64	43	20	49	$1,192,190
Randall R. Russell	386	48	53	49	13	39	$409,732
Shane M. Spiess	314	41	46	58	13	45	$479,438
Ronald D, Allen Sr.	154	34	27	12	22	47	$630,583

The racing season for the trainers of Great Lakes Downs begins and ends with the name Bennett. Whether you check the form and see the father, Gerald S. Bennett, or the son, Dale Bennett, the odds are that you're starting with one leg-up on your analysis. Now add to the equation Denise Bennett and you have a formidable start of a trifecta. In case you have a quandary, you can always find a member of the family down in Florida during the winter, because they are all regulars on the winter circuit at Gulfstream, Calder, and Tampa Bay Downs.

♣ MEET LEADING JOCKEYS FOR 2006

NAME	STARTS	1ST	2ND	3RD	WIN %	$ %	PURSES
T. D. Houghton	724	185	132	97	26	57	$1,893,874
Mary Elizabeth Doser	526	104	85	82	20	52	$1,147,973
Mike Allen	426	79	76	55	19	49	$937,734
Jareth Loveberry	607	67	80	71	11	36	$632,101
Luis Jeronimo Martinez	329	54	45	59	16	48	$504,372
Felipe J. Santos	438	52	56	79	12	43	$544,328

While T. D. Houghton seemed to once again finish in the money in excess of 50 percent of the time, he again had a fight to the finish with Mary Doser, who also exceeded 50 percent. Although Mary Doser had been on fire during Great Lakes' inaugural season (1999), in which she won the riding title at Great Lakes as well as leading female jockey in the nation, she also has been placed among the top three leading female jockeys in jockey standings for 2000 and 2001, and having scored six wins on a single card.

Great Lakes is the typical starter track for female jockeys. While many have begun their racing careers there, most have ventured out to points east and west of Michigan.

In chapter two I briefly mentioned the use of apprentice jockeys. Since weight is a very important factor, especially with regard to young horses, when analyzing a race card, consideration should be given to these young jockeys. At Great Lakes Downs, the 2006 name in apprentice jockeys was Jareth Loveberry.

When looking at his intangibles, Loveberry gains points for riding mounts both here and at Beulah Park in Ohio. Incidentally, Beulah Park is one of the feeder tracks for Great Lakes. The 2007 season will tell the tale, since Loveberry has now lost his apprentice weight allowance and must compete heads-up against the other journeyman riders for mounts.

There are times when you can suffer from a "paralysis of analysis." It was closing day at Great Lake Downs and I decided that after looking at the complete card, I only found one race that I felt comfortable with.

If I haven't said it before, let me say it now. Each track is about as different as every race. And before we start the analysis of race

cards from Great Lakes, there is one factor that is extremely important to remember. Since the track is only a five-eighths oval, the
distance from the last turn to the finish line is only 580 feet. This
single factor then places a premium on front-end speed and positioning. So when you look at the first quarter times of :22 or :23
seconds as compared to the final times of 1:14, you can see that the
up-front speed tends to take a heavy toll and burnout any final
stamina at six furlongs.

Sometimes in the process of analysis, there are things like weight
that might make you take a pause. One such situation is when a horse
has been winning with an apprentice, but the race that you're analyzing includes a 10-pound weight change at a distance and class that
he has won before.

It is at times like these when I think of one of the greatest weight
carriers ever. His name was Forego. Forego was foaled in 1970, the
same year as Secretariat. While the young Secretariat showed championship potential as soon as he started to grow, Forego was achieving
an awesome reputation as an unmanageable rogue. The huge colt displayed an ungentlemanly interest in fillies, and he had the painful and
dangerous habit of savaging with his teeth any human who came near
him. In desperation, his owner, Mrs. Edward Gerry of the Lazy F
Ranch, had him gelded.

Gelding eventually made him trainable, but Forego didn't get to
the races until age three. He broke his maiden on the second try and
added credible second-place finishes in the Hutchenson Stake and the
Florida Derby, but was a distant fourth as a 28-to-1 shot in Secretariat's
record-smashing Kentucky Derby triumph in 1973. Not until the fall,
with convincing victories in Aqueduct's Roamer and Discovery
Handicaps, did Forego begin to show signs of greatness.

That supreme talent was apparent right from the beginning of
Forego's four-year-old campaign, which he opened with four straight
stake victories. The handsome bay, at seventeen hands (who was

impossible to miss even in a crowd of horses) began to win widespread affection from the crowd that loved his thrilling late charges. Horsemen were in awe of Forego's incredible versatility. At the end of 1974, he won the one-and-a-half-mile Woodward Stake by a neck, then came back three weeks later to beat the best sprinters in the nation by three-and-a-half lengths in the seven-furlong Vosburgh Handicap. Three weeks later, he rolled to a smashing victory over a fine field of distance horses in the grueling two-mile Jockey Club Gold Cup. At the end of this campaign, Forego won three Eclipse Awards: Best Older Horse or Gelding, Best Sprinter, and, of course, Horse of the Year.

Forego followed with two more Horse of the Year campaigns in 1975 and 1976. In both years, he won two legs of the Handicap Triple Crown, the second year losing the coveted honor in the Suburban Handicap by a heart-breaking nose to Foolish Pleasure. That 1976 campaign was capped, however, by one of the most remarkable victories in racing history in the Marlboro Cup. Honest Pleasure, carrying eighteen pounds less than Forego's hefty 137-pound impost, moved out to a huge lead in the one-and-a-quarter-mile contest. At the top of the stretch, Forego looked totally out of the race, but jockey Bill Shoemaker moved the huge gelding out into the middle of the sloppy track. Forego started to gobble up lengths in an astounding stretch run that ended with him sticking a head in front in the last stride.

Two years later, Forego was finally forced into retirement by a bad left ankle that had plagued him throughout his entire career. He finished just $40,000 short of passing Kelso to head the all-time money-winning list.

Take for example the race card for November 1, 2006:

♣ GREAT LAKES DOWNS, NOVEMBER 1, 2006—RACE 1

STAKE Michigan Futurity - For Thoroughbred Two Year Old Colts and Geldings (S)
Seven Furlongs On The Dirt/Purse: $48,000 Added.

PN	ENTRY	JOCKEY	WEIGHT	MED.
7	Lite Legacy	Allen, Mike	119	L
3	Fortunate Sun	Moilna, Tommy	119	L
5	Born to Tango	Houghton, Timothy	119	L bf
1A	Oberelp	Santos, Felipe	119	1
2	Armored Truck	Doser, Mary	119	L b
4	Spirituality	Loveberry, Jareth	119	L
1	Furka Pass	Mata, Fedenco	119	L b
6	Dan Little Man	Martinez, Luis	119	

PN	ENTRY	SPEED	CLASS	DISTANCE	STYLE	INTANGIBLES	TOTAL
1	Furka Pass	5	6	7	6		24
2	Armored Truck	6	7	6	7		26
3	Fortunate Sun	9	9	8	9		35
4	Spirituality	7	8	5	8		28
5	Born to Tango	8	10	9	10		37
6	Dan Little Man	3	4	6	5		18
7	Lite Legacy	10	9	10	8		37

PN	ENTRY	WIN	PLACE	SHOW
7	Lite Legacy	16.20	8.00	5.80
3	Fortunate Sun - Q		4.20	5.00
5	Born to Tango			6.00

EXACTA	54.20

Since the Allen-Allen combination had gone 60 percent in the money all season, and although Lite Legacy, on paper, looked like a horse that couldn't find his way back to the barn in anything from 5 to 6 furlongs, I looked to see what his closing fractions were. Sure as shooting, on paper, the longer he ran, the better he got. So I boxed the 3-5-7 as an exacta, figuring that the Allen-Allen combo should get third money.

♣ GREAT LAKES DOWNS, NOVEMBER 1, 2006—RACE 4

CLAIMING - For Three Year Old and Upward Fillies and Mares (NW2 9M)/Claiming Price: $4,000/Six Furlongs On The Dirt Track/Purse: $5,400.

PN	ENTRY	JOCKEY	WEIGHT	MED.
4	Rainbow Rose	Doser, Mary	123	L
6	Best Offer	Santos, Felipe	120	L b
3	Ittybittybeau	Houghton, Timothy	120	L bf
1	Lake Station	Loveberry, Jareth	120	L b
10	Brigadoon	Mata, Federico	123	L
2	Satin Black	Molina, Tommy	120	L bf
5	Importantbusiness	Alcala, Natividad	115	L
7	Hilda Browne	Martinez, Luis	115	L b
9	Glamorize	Hannlgan, Lyndon	118	L b
8	Its Golden	Allen, Mike	115	L bf

PN	ENTRY	SPEED	CLASS	DISTANCE	STYLE	INTANGIBLES	TOTAL
1	Lake Station	7	8	7	8		30
2	Satin Black	6	7	6	7		26
3	Ittybittybeau	10	8	8	9		35
4	Rainbow Rose	9	9	9	10		37
5	Importantbusiness	5	6	5	6		22
6	Best Offer	8	10	10	8		36
7	Hilda Browne	6	6	6	6		24
8	Its Golden	5	5	4	5		19
9	Glamorize	4	4	4	5		17
10	Brigadoon	6	7	6	7		26

PN	ENTRY	WIN	PLACE	SHOW
4	Rainbow Rose	6.60	3.80	2.60
6	Best Offer		5.60	3.40
3	Ittybittybeau			3.80

EXACTA	39.80	TRIFECTA	165.00

In this race Rainbow Rose and Mary Doser, on paper, looked like Halle Berry and Billy Bob Thornton in the movie Monster's Ball and I was hoping for that kind of action. There would be only two other horses that she would have to hold off—Ittybittybeau, with Houghton aboard, and Best Offer, ridden by the pesky Felipe Santos, who closed in his last race like a hound dog chasing a bone. Since this was closing day, I played it safe and my investment was 3-4-6 in the exacta and trifecta boxed.

♣ GREAT LAKES DOWNS, NOVEMBER 1, 2006—RACE 5

MAIDEN CLAIMING - For Thoroughbred Three Year Old and Upward Fillies and Mares/Claiming Price: $5,000/Six Furlongs On The Dirt/Purse: $5,000.

PN	ENTRY	JOCKEY	WEIGHT	MED.
1	Sheisastar	Doser, Mary	116	L b
3	Konlin	Deonauth, Kenneth	118	L b
6	Search N Seize	Loveberry, Jareth	116	
2	Miss Monarch	Houghton, Timothy	116	L b
4	Broadway Park	Spanabel, Kelly	121	L
5	Lets Go Maria	Allen, Mike	116	
8	Four O'Clock	Mate, Fedenco	116	L
10	Can't We Smooch	Hannigan, Lyndon	121	L b
7	Maria Gulch	Jessup, Timothy	118	L b

PN	ENTRY	SPEED	CLASS	DISTANCE	STYLE	INTANGIBLES	TOTAL
1	Sheisastar	10	9	10	9		38
2	Miss Monarch	7	7	7	7		28
3	Konlin	9	10	9	10		38
4	Broadway Park	6	5	6	5		22
5	Lets Go Maria	5	6	5	6		22
6	Search N Seize	8	8	8	8		32
7	Maria Gulch	4	4	4	4		16
8	Four O'Clock	6	6	6	6		24
10	Can't We Smooch	5	5	5	5		20

PN	ENTRY	WIN	PLACE	SHOW
1	Sheisastar	4.00	2.80	2.10
3	Konlin		9.60	3.80
6	Search N Seize			2.40

EXACTA	33.80	TRIFECTA	99.20

Sometimes the best-laid plans do get mixed up, and I can't really take any credit for this race because I made a mistake that turned out to be right. All right, get off my back—sometimes it's better to be lucky rather than good. Here is what happened. I was placing bets at two different tracks when I misplaced my glasses and placed the bets on the wrong tracks. When I realized my mistake, at first I wanted to call up and change it, but then I thought, 'Hell, I deserve the loss because of my stupidity. So be a chump and let it ride.' You could imagine my surprise when I heard the results. Oh, by the way, my original bet was Sheisastar (1), Miss Monarch (2), and Broadway Park (4). Needless to say, the bet I placed on a race in California was a loser. Hell, for all I know they might still be running.

♣ GREAT LAKES DOWNS, NOVEMBER 1, 2006—RACE 6

CLAIMING - For Three Year Olds and Upward--Fillies and Mares/
Claiming Price: $4,000/Six Furlongs On The Dirt/Purse: $5,800

PN	ENTRY	JOCKEY	WEIGHT	MED.
3	Pottawatamie	Houghton, Timothy	115	L
10	Cant Waft	Doser, Mary	120	L
9	St Beauty	Jessup, Timothy	120	L b
8	PeppermintGift	Santos, Felipe	114	L b
2	Tickle Bug	Mata, Fedenco	118	L
1	Thy Facts	Trimble, Patricia	115	L bf
6	So Fong	Allen, Mike	120	L
5	AlysGoodoeed	Hannigan, Lyndon	120	Lb
7	Stellaspeech	Loveberry, Jareth	117	L
4	Sweet Miriam	Martinez, Luis	120	L b

PN	ENTRY	SPEED	CLASS	DISTANCE	STYLE	INTANGIBLES	TOTAL
1	Thy Facts	6	6	6	6		24
2	Tickle Bug	7	7	7	7		28
3	Pottawatamie	9	9	9	9		36
4	Sweet Miriam	4	4	4	4		16
5	AlysGoodoeed	5	5	5	5		20
6	So Fong	6	5	6	5		22
7	Stellaspeech	4	5	6	5		20
8	PeppermintGift	7	6	5	7		25
9	Shining Beauty	10	8	8	8		34
10	Can't Waft	8	10	10	10		38

PN	ENTRY	WIN	PLACE	SHOW
3	Pottawatamie	12.60	5.20	4.60
10	Can't Waft		4.80	4.00
9	Shining Beauty			33.80

EXACTA	74.80	TRIFECTA	1,589.00

People have a tendency to discredit tips on horses. I must admit I'm not one of them. But let me clarify my statement. The tip must come from someone who knows the track and has made money there. Pottawatamie had been racing at the Downs all season and, at best, could be called a bridesmaid. Even without the tip, I would have put her in the exacta and the trifecta anyway. But I never would have thought that she could win. At best, I saw her in the money, even with Houghton in the irons. To look at my analysis, I saw Can't Waft as a "can't lose" horse to beat. On paper it seemed like another classic battle between two jockeys—Houghton and Doser. But what I really found strange was that jockey Timothy Jessup on Shining Beauty was being treated like a Mars Bar in the swimming pool. It seemed to me that a horse with this kind of speed would hang in there in order to get a piece. Sure there was So Fong, but after her last race on October 9th, I had written that this horse needed a rest. Hell, I had burned quite a few dollars on her before and I thought enough was enough.

CHAPTER FOUR

Lone Star Park

FOR YEARS WHEN people spoke of thoroughbred racing in Texas, there was only one name—Sam Houston. Prior to 2005, Lone Star Park was best described as being the Avis surrounded by a world that was pretty much owned by Hertz. Although they tried harder, none but the true racing fans even cared about the little track in Grand Prairie, Texas.

Lone Star opened in 1997 and was bought by Magna Entertainment in October 2002.

It was 2004 and one of the most important years in Lone Star Park history. Lone Star Park officially opened when the Grand Prairie, Texas, racetrack began its 63-day Spring Thoroughbred Season at 6:35 p.m. (CT). But the first time I ever really paid attention to the track was the fall of 2004 when Lone Star Park hosted an international audience of about 50,000 for the Breeders' Cup World Thoroughbred Championships, or, as some refer to it, horse racing's traveling year-end championship, because they ventured to the Southwest for the first time. This feat was the first of many that Lone Star was to pull off that weekend. The track was built to accommodate 20,000; it was expanded to accommodate 50,000.

According to the local chamber of commerce, the presence of the Breeders' Cup did pay off. It had an economic impact of adding about

$52 million to the Dallas–Fort Worth area. Since the start of the year, wagering on simulcast races was up $2 million, or 4 percent, from comparative figures in 2003. More than 35,000 Breeders' Cup seats, which for the general public ranged from $25 to $125, sold out immediately.

Racing in Texas is about as shifting as sand on the beach. The top ten trainers haven't changed their order of finish in the past three years, nor does their standing change during the spring and fall meetings.

The racing season for 2006 was conducted in two segments: from April 13 through July 23 (66 days) and October 6 through December 2 (32 days). The numbers for the fall meet are insignificant, so I have combined them with the spring meet.

Sometimes certain tracks, in their attempt to assist the betting public, dispense a plethora of information concerning the prior racing season. Lone Star was one of the tracks that did. Their Marketing Department published a press release entitled "2006 Spring Thoroughbred Season Leaders & Other Miscellaneous Statistics Seasonal Leaders."

♣ **2006 SPRING THOROUGHBRED SEASON LEADERS**
& OTHER MISCELLANEOUS STATISTICS
SEASONAL LEADERS

Jockeys

Wins, Jockey—103, Cliff Berry (2nd local title)

Earnings, Jockey—$1,783,815, Cliff Berry (2nd local title)

Stake Wins, Jockey—8, Quincy Hamilton (equals Eddie Martin's 2003 record)

Wins, Turf, Jockey—29, Quincy Hamilton

Wins, 2-year-olds, Jockey—16, Cliff Berry

Win Percentage, Jockey (mm. 50 mounts)—24.6 percent, Cliff Berry (103-for-418)

Top 3 Percentage, Jockey (mm. 50 mounts)—56.7 percent, Cliff Berry (237-for-418)

Highest Average Win Payoff, Jockey (mm. 10 wins)—$36.70, Filemon Rodriguez (16-for-311)

Mounts, Jockey—424, Quincy Hamilton

Wins, Apprentice Jockey—21, Jorge Guzman (most since Josh Boyd's record 33 wins in 2000)

Trainers

Wins, Trainer—55, Steve Asmussen (8th local title)

Earnings, Trainer—$1,336,751, Steve Asmussen (8th local title)

Stake Wins, Trainer -7, Steve Asmussen

Wins, Turf, Trainer—12, John Locke'

Wins, 2-year-olds, Trainer—13, Bret Calhoun

Win Percentage, Trainer (min. 50 starters)—31.3 percent, Cody Autrey (51-for-163—3rd straight Spring

Top 3 Percentage, Trainer (min. 50 starters)—62.6 percent, Cody Autrey (102-for-163 3rd straight Spring TB Season)

High Average Win Payoff, Trainer (min. 10 wins)—$16.40,
  Brent Davidson (12-for-113)
Starters, Trainer—244, Steve Asmussen

High Mutuels
$2 Win—$166.60, Hadiftreasure, April 16, Race 2
$2 Exacta—$1,300.00, April 16, Race 2
$2 Quinella—$660.00, June 24, Race 5
$2 Trifecta—$18,955.80, June 24, Race 5
10-cent Superfecta—$18,748.29, May 12, Race I
$2 Double—$1,085.80, April 30, Races 8–9
$2 Pick 3—$4,925.00, July 20, Races 7–9
50-cent Pick 4—$10,608.80, May 25, Races 6–9

Top Daily Racing Form Beyer Speed Figures of the Meet
111, Magnum (May 29 Lone Star Park Handicap)
109, Texcess (May 29 Lone Star Park Handicap)
101, Real Dandy
99, Kip Deville (April 29 Grand Prairie Turf Challenge)
99, Preachinatthebar (April 29 Texas Mile)

Most Decisive Victories of the Meet
13¾ lengths, Chasen (May 14 Mc110000)
12¾ lengths, Young Royalty (April 21 Mc130000)
12¾ lengths, Cosporosity (April 22 Mc120000)
12 lengths, Southern Humour (April 15 Tx-MdSpWt)
12 lengths, Foxwood Annie (July 9 C1m10000nw3/L)

Largest $2 Win Payoffs of the Meet
$166.20, Hadiftreasure (April 16 Tx-Mcl10000)
$146.40, Ciens Storm (July 20 Dm10000)

$99.40, Little Stevie (July 7 Tx-Mchnl0000)
$95.00, Dashin' Daniel (June 10 Clm4000)
$80.20, Goldon (July 13 Aoc26000nw2/x)

Jockeys: Multi-Win Days
5 wins, Cliff Berry (April 15 and June 9)
4 wins, Cliff Berry (April 19, May 6, June 2, June 16, July 1, and
  July 15), Quincy Hamilton (April 28)
3 wins, Cliff Berry (June 11, July 8, and July 16), Roman Chapa
  (July 3), Quincy Hamilton (April 22, May 10, May 11, May
  25, and June 3), Alfredo Juarez Jr. (May 27 and June 10),
  Casey Lambert (June 9), Glen Murphy (April 13, June 24, and
  June 30), Luis Quinonez (May 29), Justin Shepherd (May 13),
  Jaime Theriot (April 26, April 27, July 22, and July 23)

Trainers: Multi-Win Days
4 wins, Cody Autrey (April 19), Scott Blasi (July 22) and Bret
  Calhoun (May 26 and June 9)
3 wins, Steve Asmussen (April 20 and June 3), Cody Autrey
  (April 15, June 2, June 11, and June 16), Bitt Calhoun
  (April 28)

♣ LONE STAR PARK, APRIL 13, 2006—RACE 1

STAKE Premiere S. - For Three-Year-Olds and Upward (S)/One Mile On The Dirt/
Purse: $50,000 Guaranteed.

PN	ENTRY	JOCKEY	WEIGHT	MED.
5	Senor Amigo	Murphy, Glen	116	L
2	Andanight	Rodriguez, Omar	120	L bf
10	Lightsnatcher	Therlot, Jamie	118	
6	Agrivating General	Chapa, Roman	115	
3	The Frac	Walker, Jr., Bobby	116	L
9	Rhodif	Shepherd, Justin	116	Lf
7	Corpus Sand	Hamilton, Quincy	116	L
8	Rare Cure	Taylor, Larry	120	L b
1A	Giant Bellyache	Collier, Jeremy	118	L b
4	Bullet Crane	Chirinos, Roimes	116	L b
1	Loup Longshanks	Eramia, Richard	116	L b

PN	ENTRY	SPEED	CLASS	DISTANCE	STYLE	INTANGIBLES	TOTAL
1	Loup Longshanks	9	3	3	9		24
1A	Giant Bellyache	5	4	4	5		18
2	Andanight	8	8	8	8		32
3	The Frac	7	8	7	8		30
4	Bullet Crane	4	4	4	4		16
5	Senor Amigo	7	8	7	8		30
6	Agrivating General	8	8	8	8		32
7	Corpus Sand	5	4	5	5		19
8	Rare Cure	5	6	5	6		22
9	Rhodif	6	6	6	6		24
10	Lightsnatcher	10	10	10	10		40

PN	ENTRY	WIN	PLACE	SHOW
5	Senor Amigo	11.80	6.20	5.00
2	Andanight		14.00	6.80
10	Lightsnatcher			4.20

EXACTA	139.00	TRIFECTA	1,330.40

On paper, this race appeared to be a duel to the finish line between Senor Amigo and Lightsnatcher, with the latter just being shipped in from out of town. While the betting public seemed to give little credence to Andanight's last race, where she seemed to blow her away, the field on her way to victory seemed to believe that Agrivating General's class would be the essence of her victory. My investment was 2-5-10 exacta and trifecta boxes.

♣ LONE STAR PARK, APRIL 13, 2006—RACE 4

CLAIMING - For Thoroughbred Four Year Old and Upward Claiming Price: $10,000
One And One Sixteenth Miles On The Turf
Purse: $12,000

PN	ENTRY	JOCKEY	WEIGHT	MED.
4	Popped Corn	Hamilton, Quincy	116	L b
8	Resurgence	Chapa, Roman	116	L b
5	Thirteen Colonies	Shepherd, Justin	116	L
3	Summer Stepper	Gondron, Ted	119	L b
7	Classoffiftyseven	Stanton, Terry	119	L bf
2	Kenai River	Theriot, Jamie	118	L b
9	Leo's Way	Murphy, Glen	116	L bf
1	Clod's Crypto	Rodriguez, Filemon	116	L b
6	Bokonon	Cruz, Anthony	116	L b

PN	ENTRY	SPEED	CLASS	DISTANCE	STYLE	INTANGIBLES	TOTAL
1	Clod's Crypto	3	3	3	3		12
2	Kenai River	4	4	4	4		16
3	Summer Stepper	6	6	6	6		24
4	Popped Corn	8	9	7	8	+2	32
5	Thirteen Colonies	9	8	8	7		32
6	Bokonon	5	5	5	5		20
7	Classoffiftyseven	6	6	6	6		24
8	Resurgence	10	10	9	9		38
9	Leo's Way	7	3	7	7		24

PN	ENTRY	WIN	PLACE	SHOW
4	Popped Corn	12.80	4.60	4.00
8	Resurgence		3.20	2.60
5	Thirteen Colonies			3.20

EXACTA	44.20	TRIFECTA	183.40

This is the type of race that when you complete the analysis, you can say to yourself, "What did I do wrong?" Why? Because the top three horses on paper are Popped Corn, Thirteen Colonies, and Resurgence. What I had to do was to go on to the next race before I started to rethink my analysis and start looking for things that really weren't there. In fact, I almost did when I started looking for something that would change my mind, like Summer Stepper and Classoffiftyseven. And of particular interest was the sharp showing of Classoffiftyseven in his last outing. My investment was 4-5-8 exacta and trifecta boxed.

♣ LONE STAR PARK, APRIL 13, 2006—RACE 6

ALLOWANCE - For Three and Four Year Old Fillies (SNWI X)/
Six Furlongs On The Dirt/Purse: $27,000.

PN	ENTRY	JOCKEY	WEIGHT	MED.
10	Fancie	Chirinos, Roimes	116	L b
3	Angry Angel	Walker, Jr., Bobby	122	L f
6	Physically Fit	Theriot, Jamie	122	L
7	Seadnft	Chapa, Roman	116	L
2	Super Expectations	Murphy, Glen	122	L b
5	Olmosta	Rodriguez, Omar	116	L
8	Kathryn's Life	Taylor, Larry	116	L
1	Gift of Silver	Rodriguez, Filemon	122	L
9	Baby Kayla	Eramia, Richard	122	L f
4	Quick Command	Hamilton, Quincy	116	L

PN	ENTRY	SPEED	CLASS	DISTANCE	STYLE	INTANGIBLES	TOTAL
1	Gift of Silver	4	3	4	3		14
2	Super Expectations	6	5	6	5		22
3	Angry Angel	7	7	7	8		29
4	Quick Command	3	4	3	4		14
5	Olmosta	5	6	5	6		22
6	Physically Fit	9	9	9	9		36
7	Seadnft	6	6	6	6		24
8	Kathryn's Life	5	5	5	5		20
9	Baby Kayla	3	3	3	4		13
10	Fancie	8	8	8	7		31

PN	ENTRY	WIN	PLACE	SHOW
10	Fancie	22.20	9.40	5.80
3	Angry Angel		5.40	4.20
6	Physically Fit			7.60

EXACTA	126.00	TRIFECTA	2,100.80

On paper, Quick Command appeared to be a horse that was tired. Then as I looked at her in the paddock area, she looked even worse. She had broken a sweat and looked unsettled. On the other hand, Angry Angel appeared sharp and on her toes. In her last outing, she had appeared to be the horse to beat, but by the time she made her move, she had let the leaders get away from her. Of the remaining horses in the race, Fancie appeared to be the best bet coming in at 116 pounds—that might get her a piece of this—possibly followed by Physically Fit, the other lightweight. Maybe if I'm lucky, I'll be able to pay the taxes I owe instead of filing an extension. My investment was 3-6-7-10 exacta and trifecta boxed.

♣ LONE STAR PARK, APRIL 13, 2006—RACE 8

ALLOWANCE - For Three and Four Year Old Fillies (SNW1 X)/
Six Furlongs On The Dirt/Purse: $27,000.

PN	ENTRY	JOCKEY	WEIGHT	MED.
2	She's Open Minded	Murphy, Glen	116	L
3	Lexi's Princess	Stanton, Terry	122	L b
7	Satin Halo	Gamer, Cathleen	122	L b
5	Fantasha	Shepherd, Justin	122	L
9	Memories by Night	Ignacio, Rodolfo	122	L bf
8	Betty Garr	Gondron, Ted	119	L b
1	Frontera Cat	Walker, Jr., Bobby	122	L f
10	Fast Moment	Hamilton, Quincy	116	L
4	Slewpys Star	Taylor, Larry	116	L
6	Queen Itron	Chirinos, Roimes	122	L b

PN	ENTRY	SPEED	CLASS	DISTANCE	STYLE	INTANGIBLES	TOTAL
1	Frontera Cat	3	4	3	4		14
2	She's Open Minded	10	10	10	10		40
3	Lexi's Princess	9	9	9	9		36
4	Slewpys Star	4	5	4	5		18
5	Fantasha	2	4	5	4		15
6	Queen Itron	7	7	7	7		28
7	Satin Halo	8	8	8	8		32
8	Betty Garr	6	6	6	6		24
9	Memories by Night	5	5	5	5		20
10	Fast Moment	4	4	4	4		16

PN	ENTRY	WIN	PLACE	SHOW
2	She's Open Minded	6.60	3.80	2.80
3	Lexi's Princess		12.00	8.60
7	Satin Halo			8.40

EXACTA	111.60	TRIFECTA	1,084.80

She's Open Minded, based upon her last race, appeared to be the front-end speed. Although Fast Moment did have speed, it didn't appear that her speed in this call of competition would be able to hold up. Frontera Cat had a history of pressing the pace early at this distance, only to fall back mid-race. Conversely, Lexi's Princess, by all indication, appeared to be an off-the-pace strong closer. As for Betty Garr, her record also shows an ability to make her move mid-race, but she could not maintain it, while Satin Halo moves up in the standing, due solely to jockey Cathleen Garner, who is a strong come-from-off-the-pace jockey.

Mars Blackmon was a character that made his debut in the film *She's Gotta Have It*, created by film director and sports fan Spike Lee. He was resurrected for a Nike commercial back in 1988. The punch line to the character was when he said, "It's the shoes." In horse racing, the shoe is an important part of the betting equation. But just like those of humans, shoes come in a variety of styles, shapes, and sizes, and the same shoe can have different names in different parts of the country. There are some tracks where the word "shoe" is not even used; it's called a "plate."

All the equipment used by a racehorse is designed not for repose or opulence, but rather for lightness and efficiency. Strange as it may seem, the first aluminum horseshoes of the type nailed to hooves were fashioned by Tiffany & Co. Although the ancient Celts invented the nailed-on metal horseshoe in about 450 B.C. (an invention as revolutionary at the time as the pneumatic tire was for the automobile), it was Pierre Lorillard, owner of the renowned Rancocas Stud of the late nineteenth century, who had the brilliant idea that if he could have his horses shod in a light metal, they would be able to run faster. He ordered Tiffany & Co. to make shoes for him out of the new wonder metal, aluminum, which was still very expensive. The use of aluminum lightened each shoe by an ounce and a half. The new method was so effective that when the price of aluminum decreased, it became the standard material used to make "racing plates."

♣ TYPES OF RACING PLATES

Front: The front or plain horseshoe is a standard plate fashioned with a "toe" and used on a fast or dry track.

Outer Rim Front: A variety of the front shoe. It has a "grab" around the outer rim to keep a horse standing level and to reduce hoof shock. It can be used on either the turf or the dirt.

Jar Calk: A shoe used on the front hooves for muddy and sloppy tracks.

Mud Calk: A plate with a "toe" and a sharp "sticker" on the heel, which gives a horse a better grip or tread on a muddy track.

Block Heel: A shoe constructed with raised blocks behind and used to prevent horses from running down on their heels and to prevent slipping.

Inner Rim Front and Inner Rim Block Heel: These plates are used to keep a horse standing level at all times and are excellent plates on the grass.

Block Heel Sticker: A plate that prevents horses from running down on their heels and at the same time incorporates the features of the mud calk.

Most horses wear four standard racing plates, each one weighing about two ounces. A groove running along the centerline of each shoe helps to provide traction. The front shoes are fitted close against the foot and are a bit short of the edges of the heels to keep the shoes from being wrenched off. The hind shoes are set slightly back from the toe to prevent injury caused by striking the back of a foreleg with a hind foot while running.

Although the track is muddy, the horse is not wearing calks. By law, mud calks—which are attached to shoes to dig in and give the foot extra grip on slippery surfaces—may be only a quarter-inch long.

Many trainers never use mud calks because they feel that their potential to damage a joint or tendon outweighs the good those plates may do by providing traction. It is of interest to note that Temperence Hill, the 1980 Belmont Stake winner, 53-to-1 long-shot, was the only horse that ran the race in calks.

This is one of those parts of the equation that isn't often mentioned; however, some tracks do list this on their Internet page under the title "scratches and changes."

♣ CURRENT MEET LEADING TRAINERS (FROM 10/06/2006 TO 11/12/2006)

NAME	STARTS	1ST	2ND	3RD	WIN %	$ %	PURSES
John S. Buchanan	48	14	08	04	29	54	$220,378
Judd S. Kearl	78	12	15	14	15	53	$99,893
Toby Keeton	40	08	13	04	20	63	$47,895
Eddie D. Willis	32	08	07	05	25	63	$124,486

While the trainer pool is about as consistent as a cigar store Indian, the jockey pool—once you pass the top three (Williams, Brook, and Hernandez) is about as wide-open as a kid with a pocket of pennies standing in front of a gumball machine.

♣ CURRENT MEET LEADING JOCKEYS

NAME	STARTS	1ST	2ND	3RD	WIN %	$ %	PURSES
Jeff Williams	111	22	14	16	20	47	$155,224
James Norman Brooks	164	21	25	26	13	44	$151,640
Fidencio M. Hernandez	111	20	07	11	18	34	$83,042

Lone Star Park is the kind of track where you can find comfort in betting "overlays." An overlay is when a horse is listed at much higher odds in relation to his competitors than he should be. Sometimes the past performances of a horse that is being shipped in from a different track show that the respective horse has not displayed any special skills or even familiarity with the race classification.

Another factor besides track and weather conditions that can affect final time is the manner in which the race is run. A horse that sprints to an early lead and hugs the rail all the way to the wire is obviously going to have a faster final time than the horse that runs into traffic and has to swing wide to win.

Comparing times at different distances is another complicated problem. Flow, for example. Does the time of one horse at a mile and a sixteenth compared to that of another horse at a mile and seventy yards or that of a third at a mile and an eighth? "Parallel Time Charts" that claim to make these comparisons often ignore the rather substantial differences between tracks and day-to-day track conditions.

Finally, determining the exact time for horses finishing behind the winner depends on the speed of the horses and the distance of the race. The oft-repeated rule of thumb is that one-fifth of a second equals one length but, in fact, a horse that covers six furlongs in 1:12 covers an average of six lengths in one second, not five.

To assist handicappers in making some sense out of final times, the *Daily Racing Form* began to compute a "speed rating" system for the past performances of each horse. To arrive at this rating, the *Form* uses one hundred points as the numerical rating for the track record at each distance. For every fifth of a second a horse runs slower than the track record, the paper deducts one point. For example, the winner of a six-furlong race at Arlington Park finishes in 1:10. This time is one and three-fifths seconds, or eight-fifths of a second, slower than the track record time of 1:08 2/5. Thus, the winner's speed rating would be 100-8, or 92. For horses that finish behind the winner, the traditional one-length-equals-a-fifth-of-a-second (or one point) formula is used.

This system is so crude, however, as to be of little value. Speed ratings are of no use in comparing races at different tracks because the track records vary so widely. Because average horses run closer to track records at shorter distances than at long distances, these simple speed ratings have limited value in comparing the speed of horses at different distances. Furthermore, speed rating doesn't account for the substantial changes in racing conditions from day to day.

To compensate for this final deficiency, the *Daily Racing Form* lists a "track variant" for each racing day in its Eastern editions. This variant is computed by averaging the difference between the final times and the track records for all races run on one day. For example, if the average difference was three seconds below the track records, the track variant, at one point for each fifth of a second, would be twelve.

Unfortunately, this variant is even more misleading than the speed rating. The major problem is that the difference between final and track record times depends on the quality of races run that day and on the distance of those races. Only very low or very high ratings indicate that the track was particularly fast or slow on a given day.

For all of the reasons above, the average race-goer should concentrate on other factors besides final time when handicapping from past performances. The extraordinary success achieved in recent years by speed handicappers, however, has proven that final times can be used to compare horses. These speed handicappers analyze past performances to prepare their own speed ratings and track variants. Their computations are very time-consuming and complicated—far too complicated to go into here—and the ratings arrived at can be used successfully only by those individuals who have a sound knowledge of all factors in handicapping. Those readers interested in speed handicapping will find descriptions of this art in the books recommended at the end of this book.

Finally, there is another factor when you look at Great Lakes Downs. They have what can only be called sprint races. At Lone Star Park races go a distance of 550 yards and 870 yards, so particular care should be given to the speed.

♣ LONE STAR PARK, SATURDAY, NOVEMBER 4, 2006— RACE 1

CLAIMING - 3 Year Olds and Up/Claiming Price: $10,000/ 870 Yards/Purse: $4,500

PN	ENTRY	JOCKEY	WEIGHT	MED.
1	First Place Dee	Hernandez, Fidencio	125	L bk
2	Master Bixby	Guillen, Eleazar	123	L b
3	Tuffernmel	Baldillez, Roy	125	L b
4	Call Him First	Jerman, Jeff	124	L bf
5	Streakin and Passin	Brooks, James	125	L bf

PN	ENTRY	SPEED	CLASS	DISTANCE	STYLE	INTANGIBLES	TOTAL
1	First Place Dee	10	8	8	9		35
2	Master Bixby	9	9	8	8		34
3	Tuffernmel	7	6	5	5		23
4	Call Him First	8	10	7	6		31
5	Streakin and Passin	6	5	5	5		21

PN	ENTRY	WIN	PLACE	SHOW
1	First Place Dee	3.80	3.00	2.20
2	Master Bixby		7.40	3.20
5	Streakin and Passin			2.80

EXACTA	31.40	TRIFECTA	78.20

♣ LONE STAR PARK, SATURDAY, NOVEMBER 4, 2006— RACE 2

MAIDEN – For Quarter Horses 3, 4 and 5 Year Olds/550 Yards On The Dirt/
Purse: $5,500.

PN	ENTRY	JOCKEY	WEIGHT	MED.
1	Ej Outlaw	Jerman, Jeff	124	L bk
2	Chickazoom	Ramirez, Luis	125	L bf
3	The Red Priest	Vega, Jose	124	L b
4	Jess Special Love	Vallejo, Rodrigo	124	L
6	Coronas Shadow	Hernandez, Fidencio	124	b
7	Born of Dreams	Baldillez, Roy	124	L bf
8	More N More Dreams	Garcia, Gaspar	126	L bf

PN	ENTRY	SPEED	CLASS	DISTANCE	STYLE	INTANGIBLES	TOTAL
1	Ej Outlaw	10	9	8	7		34
2	Chickazoom	5	6	5	6		22
3	The Red Priest	6	5	6	5		22
4	Jess Special Love	8	7	7	9		24
6	Coronas Shadow	4	4	4	8		20
7	Born of Dreams	7	8	9	10		25
8	More N More Dreams	5	5	5	4		19

PN	ENTRY	WIN	PLACE	SHOW
1	Ej Outlaw	13.60	4.00	2.60
7	Born of Dreams		2.80	2.20
4	Jess Special Love			2.20

EXACTA	46.00	TRIFECTA	76.80

Examine the first two races on November 4. In the first race, First Place Dee and Streakin and Passin were the favorites, with a slight nod to First Place Dee. In winning, First Place Dee (1-2) paid $3.80; if the third place finisher Streakin and Passin (1-1) had won, he would have only paid $4.00. But what the bettors didn't look at was that Master Bixby had beaten both horses before at the same distance. Also, Master Bixby, at that distance, had what is often called a zigzag-racing pattern of win, lose, win, lose. Having just lost his last race at the distance, the bettors pushed his odds to 6-1. In this case, you box each of the two favorites with Master Bixby for a $31.40 winner.

Now in the second race, the same theory held true. Looking down at the past performances, Ej Outlaw was screaming for a victory at 550 yards but anything longer and he would have been dead meat.

♣ LONE STAR PARK, APRIL 13, 2006—RACE 3
Maiden/Special Weight/Six Furlongs/Purse: $25,000.

PN	ENTRY	JOCKEY	WEIGHT	MED.
10	Open Meadows	Lambert, Casey	117	L bf
4	Shezmorethanready	Taylor, Larry	116	L
5	Formal Legend	Chapa, Roman	116	L
11	Fashion Creek	Therlot, Jamie	122	L b
8	Enchanted Landing	Walker, Jr., Bobby	116	L b
2	Mama Panchita	Murphy, Glen	122	L
1	Mark Me An Angel	Rodnguez, Filemon	116	L b
7	Vera Rose	Ignacio, Rodolfo	116	L
13	Govenor's Ully	Eramia, Richard	122	L b
12	Diva de Amante	Stanton, Terry	116	b
6	Green Light Baby	Shepherd, Justin	122	L
3	Olmos Ivy	Rodriguez, Omar	122	L b

PN	ENTRY	SPEED	CLASS	DISTANCE	STYLE	INTANGIBLES	TOTAL
10	Open Meadows	9	8	9	10		36
4	Shezmorethanready	8	9	9	9		35
5	Formal Legend	7	7	6	8		28
11	Fashion Creek	6	6	7	7		26
8	Enchanted Landing	5	5	5	6		21
2	Mama Panchita	3	4	5	8		20
1	Mark Me An Angel	4	4	4	7		19
7	Vera Rose	4	4	4	7		19
13	Govenor's Ully	2	5	6	5		18
12	Diva de Amante	2	5	3	7		17
6	Green Light Baby	1	3	6	6		16
3	Olmos Ivy	1	5	5	5		15

PN	ENTRY	WIN	PLACE	SHOW
10	Open Meadows	5.60	2.60	2.80
4	Shezmorethanready		2.60	2.40
5	Formal Legend			2.10

EXACTA	18.40	TRIFECTA	47.60

When I stared to analyze this race, there were only five horses that I even considered. On paper and in the paddock, Open Meadow appeared to be ready—the only question I had here was his ability to make the lead without expending too much energy. If he didn't burn out, he would be able to go all the way. If not, the next best thing would have probably been Shezmorethanalady, who could take the race. I know that this is sheer chalk, but an early glance said there's nobody else other than the third place favorite Formal Legend. The investment was 4-5-10 boxed exacta and trifecta.

The race also showed me to make a note that Fashion Creek should win next time out in this class group. Guess what? He did and paid $14.20.

♣ LONE STAR PARK, APRIL 13, 2006—RACE 7

CLAIMING - For Four Year Olds and Upward/Claiming Price: $15,000/
Five Furlongs On The Turf/Purse: $15,000.

PN	ENTRY	JOCKEY	WEIGHT	MED.
4	Tricky Storm	Taylor, Larry	116	L
10	Calling Randy	Thelot, Jamie	119	L bf
1	I'm A Consultant	Shepherd, Justin	122	L
5	Sabre Rattling	Rodriguez, Filemon	116	L b
8	Gambler's Share	Murphy, Glen	116	L
7	Merri's Sella	Stanton, Terry	116	L b
1A	Jer Dandy	Eramia, Richard	116	L
3	Hamaaly	Rodriguez, Jesus	118	L b
6	RichIe Cee	Hamilton, Quincy	116	L b

PN	ENTRY	SPEED	CLASS	DISTANCE	STYLE	INTANGIBLES	TOTAL
1	I'm A Consultant	8	8	8	8		32
1A	Jer Dandy	8	8	8	8	-1 LESSER OF ENTRY	31
3	Hamaaly	7	7	7	7		28
4	Tricky Storm	10	10	10	10		40
5	Sabre Rattling	6	6	6	6		24
6	RichIe Cee	5	5	5	5		20
7	Merri's Sella	4	4	4	4		16
8	Gambler's Share	3	3	3	3		12
10	Calling Randy	9	9	9	9		36

PN	ENTRY	WIN	PLACE	SHOW
4	Tricky Storm	4.20	2.80	2.60
10	Calling Randy		6.40	3.80
1	I'm A Consultant			3.00

EXACTA	24.80	TRIFECTA	103.20

Tricky Storm is the speed of the race and should be able to hold on over Jamie Thelot, who should be fast closing with Calling Randy for second or third over the entry of Jer Dandy and I'm a Consultant, so my investment was to box 1-10-4 in both the exacta and trifecta.

The one thing that you will consistently find is that the overlays at Lone Star Park are there for the taking. The fact is that you have to look.

CHAPTER FIVE

Turf Paradise

EARLY IN 2007, I decided to make a change and include a fourth track in my daily analysis. Having kept an eye on the Turf Paradise facility for the past three months, I've decided to add this track to my winter racing program.

To provide some background, Turf Paradise opened its doors on January 7, 1956. Since that day, Phoenicians—Phoenix residents— appear to have "taken" to Thoroughbred racing. Throughout the season, they are filling every seat and standing shoulder-to-shoulder to welcome pari-mutuel racing to Arizona—the Valley's first sports franchise.

In the early years, the track was the frequent home to celebrities like Jackie Gleason and Joe E. Brown. And while Gleason never seemed to find a race he didn't want to bet on, Brown seemed to always be on a mission to find cheap claimers that he could ship to California.

The new millennium provided Turf Paradise with a new owner, Jerry Simms. This self-made multimillionaire purchased Turf Paradise on June 16, 2000 for $53 million. Mixing business insight and know-how entrepreneurship, Simms had Midas-touched modest investments in southern California automobile dealerships, residential and commercial real-estate ventures, and banking into fortunes. Simms immediately set out a $5 million renovation plan designed to enhance the racing experience with a quality dining and entertainment ambience. Both the

Clubhouse and Turf Club were completely renovated and re-styled in an elegant and comfortable décor. Two race-book-style betting nooks— one has been placed in the Clubhouse and the other is adjacent to the Turf Club—plus eighty private terminals were added.

Simms also had the main track and turf course renovated. Then in the summer of 2003, Simms built a $125,000 equine swimming pool in the stable area of the racetrack. The thirty-by-sixty-foot pool offers state-of-the-art horse therapy for the over 2,200 Thoroughbreds stabled on the backside. It contains over 140,000 gallons of water; it is twelve feet deep, which allows it to accommodate up to six horses simultaneously. The pool had an immediate effect, not only on equine health, but on field size, which is now averaging eight horses per race.

When analyzing their racing cards, you'll find that Turf Paradise presents a unique set of problems. The first thing, although obvious, is the weather. You are in the desert, and I don't care how much water you use to wet down the track, front-end speed seems to rule. It is a common occurrence to see distance horses going out in .22 seconds. True, this may be fine for six or even seven furlong races; but when going a mile or longer, oxygen and a red flag can't be far behind.

The second factor is track size. The main track is a one-mile oval, while the turf course is seven furlongs. The distance from the final turn to the finish is 990 feet.

Currently, the ownership has been looking at Polytrak. Recently, though, the surface that came to prominence down at Keeneland has started to be questioned by many of the trainers. The most prominent question seems to center around the balling-up of the surface mixture of sand, carpet fibers, rubber, and wax. It appears that many of the horses seem to be collecting the material in their hoofs and shoes, thus creating the possibility of horses hitting the racing surface unevenly.

♣ LEADING TRAINERS AT TURF PARADISE
Starting Date: 10/06/2006; Ending Date: 11/13/2006

Name	Starts	1st	2nd	3rd	Earnings
Troy Bainum	36	12	10	4	$110,416
Justin Evans	48	11	9	6	$104,683
Dan L. McFarlane	37	11	5	2	$118,123
Joe Toye	27	8	5	3	$54,500
Doug Oliver	18	7	3	2	$88,991
William L. Mehok	20	7	1	4	$57,918
Jim Hill	18	6	4	2	$33,868
David Van Winkle	27	6	2	5	$64,878
Bart G. Hone	29	5	4	4	$53,440
J. Eric Kruljac	21	5	2	3	$33,240
Edward J. Kereluk	17	5	2	1	$27,228
Molly J. Pearson	34	4	3	8	$47,986

♣ LEADING JOCKEYS AT TURF PARADISE

Name	Starts	1st	2nd	3rd	Earnings
Glenn W. Corbett	91	20	10	12	$205,750
Adolfo A. Morales	67	19	10	9	$181,583
Chris Landeros	90	18	19	15	$176,972
Scott A. Stevens	80	18	8	12	$188,965
Lorenzo Castane Lopez	104	12	22	9	$106,935
Luis Miguel Hernandez	108	12	16	19	$140,867
Kristina Kenney	86	12	6	10	$99,144
Esteban Angel Gomez	73	11	7	8	$83,130
Ry Eikleberry	68	10	10	12	$103,299
Daniel P. Vergara	67	10	5	12	$75,582
Leslie Mawing	71	9	13	5	$95,955
Hector Ventura, Jr.	60	8	11	11	$105,566
Jorge Carreno	45	8	8	4	$67,117
Alberto R. Higuera	62	6	5	3	$35,738
Juan G. Rivera	58	6	4	12	$91,853
Orlando A. Martinez	56	5	8	6	$41,704
Michael Phillip Iammarino	55	5	6	8	$52,127

The first race that I tackled was the fifth race:

♣ TURF PARADISE, JANUARY 28, 2007—RACE 5

MAIDEN CLAIMING —-Three-Years Old Fillies/Claiming Price: $12,500-$10,500/
Five and a Half Furlongs/ On The Dirt/Purse: $6,500.

PN	ENTRY	JOCKEY	WEIGHT	MED.
1	My Sis Steffie	Guerra, Vince	121	L b
2	Safe Angel	Ortiz, Jr., Ivan	121	L b
3	Potentilla	Stevens, Scott	121	L
4	Mackenzies Quick	Mawing, Leslie	121	L b
5	Craftynthefastlane	Rivera, Juan	121	L
6	Social Lady	Kato, Akifumi	121	L b
7	Siphonanna	Lopez, Lorenzo	121	L
8	Brazilada	Corbett, Glenn	121	L b
9	Steve's Girl	Landeros, Chris	116	L b

PN	ENTRY	SPEED	CLASS	DISTANCE	STYLE	INTANGIBLES	TOTAL
1	My Sis Steffie	9	9	9	9		36
2	Safe Angel	8	7	8	7		30
3	Potentilla	9	9	10	10		38
4	Mackenzies Quick	6	6	6	6		24
5	Craftynthefastlane	5	5	5	5		20
6	Social Lady	7	5	7	5		24
7	Siphonanna	6	7	6	7		26
8	Brazilada	5	6	5	6		22
9	Steve's Girl	10	10	10	10		40

PN	ENTRY	WIN	PLACE	SHOW
9	Steve's Girl	6.00	3.80	2.60
3	Potentilla		5.60	3.20
1	My Sis Steffie			2.60

EXACTA	35.40	TRIFECTA	31.70

♣ TURF PARADISE, JANUARY 28, 2007—RACE 6

MAIDEN CLAIMING –Fillies and Mares, Four-Year-Olds and Up/Six Furlongs/
Purse: $6,000.

PN	ENTRY	JOCKEY	WEIGHT	MED.
1	Regaletta	Baze, Vicky	121	L
2	It's Nippy	Martinez, Orlando	121	L
3	Lady In The Dark	Smith, Jeff	120	L
4	Rare American	Rosales, Arturo	121	L
5	Tropic Pass	Gann, Sandi Lee	120	L
6	Surely Mae	Sisco, Natasha	116	L
7	Lil Olive	Carreno, Jorge	120	L
8	Pink Halo	Ortiz, Jr., Ivan	120	
9	Barbaric Music	Dieguez, Wilson Omar	121	L
10	Miss Westchester	Matteucci, Tony	121	L
11	Textme	Corbett, Glenn	120	L

PN	ENTRY	SPEED	CLASS	DISTANCE	STYLE	INTANGIBLES	TOTAL
1	Regaletta	5	5	5	5		20
2	It's Nippy	3	6	3	6		18
3	Lady In The Dark	6	6	6	6		24
4	Rare American	7	7	7	7		28
5	Tropic Pass	8	8	8	8		32
6	Surely Mae	7	3	7	3		20
7	Lil Olive	8	4	8	4		24
8	Pink Halo	6	6	5	5		22
9	Barbaric Music	7	5	7	5		24
10	Miss Westchester	6	6	5	5		22
11	Textme	9	8	9	8		34

PN	ENTRY	WIN	PLACE	SHOW
5	Tropic Pass	5.60	3.80	2.60
4	Rare American		13.00	7.60
11	Textme			2.60

EXACTA	97.00	TRIFECTA	442.20

This race appears to be a speed dual between Textime and
Tropical Pass. On paper both appear to be knocking at the door to
break their maiden. Since the race is only six furlongs, I don't think
it's long enough for either of them to get into trouble. The only question that I have is that there is a distinct overlay. If you look at the past
performances, Rare American is the only horse that seems to find it
hard living up to both her class and potential. On paper she looks like
a definite heartbreaker. This is a situation where you need to make a

defensive bet by including this horse in your investment. Therefore, the investment is 4-5-11 in a boxed exacta and trifecta.

So far we have talked primarily about races on the dirt, but when you can find a good and fair turf race, please "have at it."

♣ TURF PARADISE, JANUARY, 29, 2007—6TH RACE

OPTIONAL CLAIMING/Six-1/2 Furlongs/4-Year-Olds and Up Maiden/
Claiming Price: $10,000/Purse: $8,200.

PN	ENTRY	JOCKEY	WEIGHT	MED.
1	The Dude Guy	Kenny, Jocelyn	121	L
2	Sax Notes	Baze, Vicky	118	L
4	Intrepid Cat	Morales, Adolfo	118	L
5	Red's Memories	Martinez, Orlando	118	L
6	Innaboutaweek	Rivera, Juan	120	L
7	American Games	Mawing, Leslie	120	L
8	Sunday Berries	Eikleberry, Ky	120	L
9	A.C. Danzer	Durigon, Joseph	119	L
10	Man of the House	Painter, Leanne	118	L

PN	ENTRY	SPEED	CLASS	DISTANCE	STYLE	INTANGIBLES	TOTAL
1	The Dude Guy	7	1	10	9		27
2	Sax Notes	8	6	6	6	-2	24
4	Intrepid Cat	2	3	7	10		22
5	Red's Memories	6	8	4	4		22
6	Innaboutaweek	3	10	8	7		28
7	American Games	10	5	5	5		25
8	Sunday Berries	5	7	3	2		21
9	A.C. Danzer	4	2	6	8		20
10	Man of the House	2	9	9	9		29

PN	ENTRY	WIN	PLACE	SHOW
10	Man of the House	4.80	3.00	3.00
6	Innaboutaweek		3.60	3.20
1	The Dude Guy			6.60

EXACTA	14.80	TRIFECTA	45.40

Here is a case where listening to the pre-race analyst can help. In this case, I had lost on the first three races, but was stymied by the past performance record of Centauri until he was scratched. Then things began to make more sense.

By March I had been watching races at Turf Paradise for three months and felt comfortable with the trainers, the jockeys, the track, the announcers, etc. By that point, I had collected a rather extensive library on many of the horses that had raced here. I realized that the largest feeder tracks were Churchill Downs and Keeneland. The only question that I had to allow for was the question of Polytrak (see above prior mention).

On March 13 I decided to see if my notes and analysis of Turf Paradise were on the money. When you start with a new track, the one thing not to do is underestimate the people who bet there daily. Don't assume that you're going to come in and teach them something new. It's sort of like "When in Rome . . . follow the Italians!"

♣ TURF PARADISE, MARCH 13, 2007—RACE 3

CLAIMING - For Three Year Olds and Upward (NW1 9MX)/Claiming Price: $3,000/
Five And One Half Furlongs On The Dirt/Purse: $6,000.

PN	ENTRY	JOCKEY	WEIGHT	MED.
4	Forest Way	Hemandez, Miguel	122	L f
1	Jade Halo	Duarte, Saul	117	b
7	Apollo Jack	Lopez, Lorenzo	122	L f
8	Skip N Go Naked	Kenney, Kristine	122	L f
3	Nab a Copy	Keith, Lad	122	L b
2	Ozoned	Banio, Anna	122	L bf
5	Proud Danny	Smith, Jeff	122	L b

PN	ENTRY	SPEED	CLASS	DISTANCE	STYLE	INTANGIBLES	TOTAL
1	Jade Halo	9	8	9	7		33
2	Ozoned	6	6	6	6		24
3	Nab a Copy	4	5	5	5		19
4	Forest Way	10	9	8	7		34
5	Proud Danny	5	4	4	4		19
7	Apollo Jack	7	7	7	7		28
8	Skip N Go Naked	3	3	3	3		12

PN	ENTRY	WIN	PLACE	SHOW
4	Forest Way	7.60	4.20	3.00
1	Jade Halo		4.00	2.40
7	Apollo Jack			2.40

EXACTA	43.20	TRIFECTA	53.50

Forest Way, which was my second favorite, had the ability to come from off the pace or take the lead. The determining factor would be how Apollo Jack was going to run. If Apollo Jack and Forest Way got into a speed duel, then my third choice would be Jade Halo to pick up the pieces. Remember, they're going only 5½ furlongs. My investment was to box the 1-4-7 in both an exacta and trifecta.

Sometimes there is a tendency to try and force the matter. Sometimes the best investment is the one that you didn't make. I looked at several races but did not bet again until the seventh race. During the repast, however, I took notes on races 4, 5, and 6.

Check Out Receipt

Harold Washington Library Center

Saturday, June 4, 2022 10:20:16 AM

Item: R0439986651
Title: Small track betting : pick more winners using this ire-fire eight-point system of race analysis
Due: 6/25/2022

Item: R0458057738
Title: Your next five moves : master the art of business strategy
Due: 6/25/2022

Total items: 2

Thank you.

912

3, 2007—RACE 7

ward-Fillies and Mares (NW3 1)/
ongs On The Dirt/Purse: $10,300.

	WEIGHT	MED.
in	119	Lf
on	121	
ne	119	L b
to	123	L
o	121	L 2
	118	Lb
o	119	L

STANCE	STYLE	INTANGIBLES	TOTAL
8	7		30
7	5		29
6	5		22
9	8		34
10	9		38
5	4		20
4	4		16

	PLACE	SHOW
	3.20	2.40
	5.20	3.00
		2.60

EXACTA	22.00	TRIFECTA	33.40

If you've been reading carefully, you have noticed that I like both trifectas and exactas. There are instances when I will venture into the land of the superfecta. With all kudos to Steve Christ, I can count on one hand the times that I do that. But when I looked at the seventh race I knew that I had to make the effort, since I only had one race left to bet on and I wanted to meet my number for the day.

As you can see from my chart, FancyGold was head-and-shoulders above the field. Carrying only 119 pounds and with speed to burn, the pre-race favorite would only pay somewhere between $4.80 and $5.20 to win. The second and third choices for the race were a toss-up between Watcher Knows and Tobin Royalty. As I looked in at the paddock area, I saw Brendy and jockey Alberto Higuera and again looked at the 123 pounds that he was carrying. While Higuera is not a household name, I had seen him before on heavyweight horses, which have finished in the money several times. Also there was the fact that Brendy was a consistent horse that needed to find a $10,000 claiming race where he could really show his ability. $16,000 horses are a real stretch for him. So the investment was a 6-1, 6-4 exacta followed by a 6-4-1, 6-1-4 trifecta, and for good measure, I played a 6-1-4-2, 6-4-1-2 superfecta.

My final race of the day was the eighth race:

♣ TURF PARADISE, MARCH 13, 2007—RACE 8

CLAIMING - For Three Year Olds and Upward/Claiming Price: $7,500/
One And One Sixteenth Miles On The Turf/Purse: $8,500.

PN	ENTRY	JOCKEY	WEIGHT	MED.
4	Mister Cosmi (GB)	Gann, Sandi	119	L b
8	Snowy River Man	Kenney, Kristine	121	L b
3	Con Say One	Dieguez, Wilson	119	L f
6	Wingbrook	Morales, Adolfo	119	L bf
7	Swelter	Von Rosen, Anne	119	L b
1	Chapel Ridge	Martinez, Orlando	119	L
5	Occupied	Elkleberry, Ry	119	L b
2	Atticus in Style	Keith, Lori	119	L b

PN	ENTRY	SPEED	CLASS	DISTANCE	STYLE	INTANGIBLES	TOTAL
1	Chapel Ridge	4	4	4	4		16
2	Atticus in Style	7	7	7	7		28
3	Con Say One	9	8	9	8		34
4	Mister Cosmi	10	9	10	9		38
5	Occupied	6	6	6	6		24
6	Wingbrook	3	3	3	3	+3	15
7	Swelter	5	5	5	5		20
8	Snowy River Man	8	10	7	10		35

PN	ENTRY	WIN	PLACE	SHOW
4	Mister Cosmi (GB)	9.40	4.60	2.80
8	Snowy River Man		2.60	2.40
3	Con Say One			5.60

EXACTA	26.20	TRIFECTA	87.60

This field of eight showed a mixture of skilled horses and imposters. First, there was the elimination of the imposters. On paper, Chapel Ridge, Swelter, and Occupied were not ready for prime-time, even at $8,500. Now left with five horses, I eliminated one of the favorites, Atticus in Style, both because he looked lethargic and, having seen jockey Lori Keith on the turf, I was not sure that she was right for the mount no matter what the past performances said. Left now with four horses, the decision was simple. The worst of the remaining four was Wingbrook. Left with Master Cosmi, Con Say One, and Snowy River Man, my investment was 4-3-8 in a boxed exacta and trifecta.

Every so often, perhaps once every fifteen or twenty years, there comes to racing a horse so perfectly conformed, so talented, and so tragic that it breaks the hearts of even the most hardened horsemen. Such a horse was the filly Ruffian.

By Reviewer and out of Shenanigans, Ruffian was huge for a filly. At age three, she stood sixteen hands, two inches. Her coat was bay and her temperament was difficult. In her eye was the "look of eagles," which had been passed down from her paternal grandsire, Bold Ruler, and her maternal grandsire, Native Dancer. According to the Belmont and Aqueduct's head veterinarian, Manuel Gilman, "She was the most perfectly put together large filly I've ever seen."

Recently, I was asked by a young racing fan to describe Ruffian. Knowing that his knowledge of racing was limited to his years on the face of the Earth, I told him I would give him an answer in human terms. I said, "In today's vernacular, she would be a result of the best of combination of the physical characteristics of Angelina Jolie, Beyonce Knowles, and Jennifer Lopez, with the mind of attorney Jamie Gorelick."

Trained by Hall of Famer Frank Whitely, Ruffian won her first ten starts with about as much ease as a hot knife goes through butter. In her first start as a two-year-old in 1974, Ruffian broke late out of the gate, but quickly made up for lost time, blazing across the finish line fifteen lengths ahead of the second-place horse, and equaling the track record for the distance (5½ furlongs). She was undefeated in her next four races, thus earning the title of Champion Two-Year-Old Filly. But victory didn't come without consequences. She sustained a hairline fracture of the right hind leg, which sidelined her until April of her three-year-old campaign, but she came back sound and full of fight.

As a three-year-old in 1975, Ruffian won five races, including the Filly Triple Crown: the Acorn Stake, the Mother Goose Stake, and the Coaching Club American Oaks. For all to see, she had proven that she was a champion, both at sprinting and at distances. It would not be until 1980 before another great filly would run against the boys. Her name was Genuine Risk. Her owners were Bert and Diane Firestone. But Ruffian created a buzz. The media was all the rage about her. So, with typical marketing hype, they invented a championship race for Ruffian and called it, "The Great Match Race."

Throughout the annals of racing lore, it must be stated that horsemen hate match races with the same venom that they hate losing. Pitting two champions against each other in head-to-head competition almost always assures that one will be run into the ground. Whitely tried to protect Ruffian's best interests, but the die was cast. And on July 6, 1975, Ruffian paraded to the post at Belmont Park to meet the champion two-year-old colt of 1974, Foolish Pleasure, over a mile-and-a-quarter distance. Foolish Pleasure, who had won eleven of his fourteen starts, had won the Derby too, but had come in second in the Preakness and the Belmont Stakes.

The two horses that broke from the gate, almost together with Foolish Pleasure, were just a hair ahead. After a few strides, Ruffian moved up beside him. They ran side by side, clocking their first quarter in 22 and a fifth seconds. Then, suddenly, jockey Jacinto Vasquez heard the horrid sound of bone cracking. Foolish Pleasure zoomed past.

Embattled and confused, Ruffian struggled on. It took Vasquez thirty strides to ease her to a halt. As Foolish Pleasure crossed the finish line to a hollow victory, an air cast was placed on Ruffian's leg and she was moved to Dr. William Reed's Veterinary Hospital across the street. The injury diagnosed was a common one—compound fracture of the sesamoid bone at the back of the fetlock joint.

Ruffian's surgery was successful, but she had such a violent reentry into consciousness that she not only destroyed all the good that had been done, but attacked the vet's assistants in her fear. Due to her mental and physical condition or the fact, as some horsemen noted, "that she was too much horse," Ruffian was humanely "put down" and buried in the Belmont infield.

Plenty of $25,000 claimers had been destroyed due to cracked sesamoids, but Ruffian was a star. Her tragedy spurred a new inquiry—an American obsession with pure speed, the viability of racetrack facilities. The American Association of Equine Practitioners put up guidelines for handling badly injured horses. New ambulances were designed. Track veterinary facilities were expanded, and many tracks discontinued the practice of specially preparing track surfaces "for world's records." New York came up with the tractor, which drags the racing strip to clear it of such objects as hoof picks, nails, and cigarette lighters, all of which can cause severe damage to horses moving at high speeds. Projects involving the proper banking of turns and more suitable racing surfaces, however, have mainly been abandoned as impractical or too expensive. Although the treatment facilities have improved, severe injury will persist until the causes of excess concussion due to unnatural speed, irregularities in the strip, and overstressing of underdeveloped bones are eliminated. Until that time comes, the enormously talented Ruffian is just another tragic statistic.

CHAPTER SIX

Tampa Bay Downs

HEARING WHISPERS ABOUT the closing of Great Lakes Downs, I began to look for a regular track to replace my Michigan sojourn and decided upon Tampa Bay Downs. I have found that if you're running a little short of money for Christmas shopping, Tampa Bay Downs can be your annual early gift from Santa. Of all the Florida racetracks, since the closing of Hialeah, Tampa Bay Downs has been one of my favorites. Besides being the little track that could, since early in the twentieth century it has been home to a collection of the most eclectic racing fans ever to wander up to a cashier's window. The motto seems to go something like, "What the hell! Let's give it a chance." Win, lose, or draw, its checkered past, present, and future has been and probably will remain about as exciting as a three-horse dead-heat finish.

Back in 1926, the track opened under the name of Tampa Downs for its inaugural meeting. Although its initial season lasted only 39 days, the ownership, headed by Ohio investor Harvey Myers and Kentucky Colonel Matt J. Winn, famed promoter of the Kentucky Derby, met with resounding success. Because of their success, Hialeah felt forced to improve purses in order to compete with Tampa Downs in the battle for horses.

Meanwhile the owners of Hialeah—James H. Bright, a rich cattleman from Missouri, and his partner, Glenn H. Curtiss, an aviation pioneer—believed that since they were the primary developers of south Florida and that they had created and developed this new city called, incidentally, Hialeah, no one was going to infringe upon their turf rights; rights that they believed stretched from the ocean to the bay.

In 1927, when Tampa Downs reopened, the Miami Jockey Club informed them that they could only operate for nine days because the remainder of the winter season had been seeded to Hialeah. This single act became the beginning of the battle for the entertainment dollar of south Florida, which continues even to today.

By 1932, the Downs had hemorrhaged so much red ink that the initial owners, who sold to Desha Breckinridge and Major Thomas McDowell of Lexington, oversaw repairs and restoration of the facility. But once again, the gang from Hialeah set up so many roadblocks that construction conflicts caused the cancellation of the meet until 1934.

In 1934 the Tampa Turf and Field Club was formed, headed by Hal Thompson. The track reopened as Tampa Downs, but, once again, inadequate handles forced the meeting to close after only six days. The facility continued to limp along until 1943, when they threw in the towel and the U.S. Army built barracks and turned the track into a jungle warfare training center.

In 1946 the Sunshine Park Racing Association was formed and provided 650 stalls. One year later, rising like the phoenix, the track was approved by referendum, and the march from oblivion was truly underway.

In 1947 this facility was credited with the start of modern racing. At that time, the track instituted and put into operation the first official tote board, an electric starting gate, and a photo finish camera. By the '50s, the track became the second home to writers covering winter baseball. In fact, the legendary sportswriters, including Grantland Rice, Red Smith, and Arthur Daley, were regulars at the track, as they traveled south to cover the baseball spring season. It was there that Grantland Rice, when referring to the facility in his many columns, coined the phase "Santa Anita of the South."

Like all patrons of the stock market who reach any modicum of success, they either consider themselves experts or they get greedy and begin to squabble with fellow stockholders. In the end, John W. Kane of Wilmington, Delaware, won control.

By 1953 the Florida legislature passed a special bill, allowing the track to keep the 15 percent takeout and, instead, to pay a $4,000 daily fee. With that single procedure, the track began to show a profit for the first time, and the new clubhouse construction began at a cost of $300,000; it was completed the following year.

With the sweet smell of success beginning to permeate the barn area, suitors came "a calling" and, in 1955, control was passed to a syndicate headed by Frederick Ballon, director of Yonkers Raceway in New York, Richard West of Rhode Island, and Frank Hobbs, a Tampa attorney.

During the course of the season, Tampa Bay is known for four major stake races.

One of the more fascinating things about Tampa racing is that sun showers pour down on one side of the track while the other side basks in complete sunshine. I have a tendency to never bet exotics in the first two races there unless something from my analysis shows some real high probability. This is one of those tracks where from right out the box, you can find yourself in a hole financially. Secondly, the possibilities of a long-shot off the form with performances with apprentice jockeys are rampant.

Tampa Bay is a track where Midwestern and Northeastern horses come with their trainers to learn how to run. It is also a place where a trainer can wean his/her horse off of medications like Lasix.

At this point, I think that you deserve to know some of the common racing ailments and injuries that racing can cause horses:

1. *Bleeding:* Some horses have a predisposition to hemorrhaging from the nostrils during or after a race or workout. The blood comes from veins ruptured in the nostrils, the pharynx, or the lungs.
2. *Bone spavin:* The formation of bony deposits on the small, flat bones at the lower part of the hock. It causes lameness.
3. *Bowed tendon:* A severe strain of one or both of the flexor tendons that run along the back of the cannon bone. Because of swelling and fluid accumulation, the tendons have a bowed appearance. This condition causes lameness and requires long rest.
4. *Bucked shins:* An inflammation of the membrane covering the front of the cannon bones of young horses, caused by excessively hard training on immature legs.
5. *Heat exhaustion:* Caused by over-exertion in hot weather. The horse stops sweating and its body temperature soars. This is often the cause of a horse collapsing after a race.
6. *Osselets:* Arthritis of the fetlock joint, which causes a hot, painful swelling.
7. *Popped knee:* A swollen knee that contains an excess of fluid; caused by an inflammation within the knee joint, often because of a bone chip.
8. *Quarter crack:* A crack found in the wall of the hoof in the area of the quarter.
9. *Ringbone:* A bony enlargement in the front and sides of the pastern.
10. *Sand crack:* A crack in the toe of the hoof.
11. *Sesanoiditis:* An inflammation of the tendon sheath covering the sesanoids, the two bones at the rear of the fetlock joint.
12. *Sinusitis:* An infection of one or both sinuses, causing breathing problems.
13. *Splints:* Young horses overworked too early often develop bone enlargements between the splint and cannon bones; they cause considerable pain.

14. *Stifle out:* This term refers to the dislocation of the stifle joint.
15. *Suspensory ligament strain:* The suspensory ligament, which runs behind the cannon bone, becomes thickened and inflamed.
16. *Whistling:* The wheezing sound made by a horse suffering from an inflammation of the respiratory tract.

Horses with chronic conditions, ailments that may act up, unhealed surgery, or soreness so marked that even numbing ice will not prevent them from limping on the track, are given the dreaded pink slips, which means they are now on the vet's list and may not race until he has seen them work out soundly. The question then becomes whether drugs are then used for therapeutic reasons or for performance-enhancement purposes. Some states permit the use of Butazolidin (an analgesic, anti-inflammatory drug) and Lasix, a drug that prevents horses from bleeding from the lungs. The theory is that when a horse feels better than it actually is, it is more likely to push itself past the limit of its capabilities and break down. It is also a fact that both "Bute" and Lasix are capable of masking the presence of other forbidden substances, such as tranquilizers and stimulants, so that they are undetectable in post-race drug tests.

Breaking down is serious. When a horse falls or even falters on the track, it is not like a basketball player breaking his ankle during a game or a tennis player dislocating her shoulder. The thirty-mile-per-hour or so momentum of the race has already been established, and the life of every horse and rider on the track is at stake.

Bute is not technically a painkiller. It reduces fever and inflammation in bones, joints, and soft tissues, thus relieving pain. Bute cannot make a horse perform any better than it would if its limbs were not inflamed, but it can make it impossible for a vet to determine whether a horse has deteriorated past the point of being a safe ride.

In 1978 the Bute controversy came to a head when a cheap claimer named Easy Edith, who was running on Bute to reduce inflammation in her left knee, shattered her cannon bone banking around the final turn of a six-furlong sprint at Pimlico. She went down, causing three other horses that were unable to stop or turn in time to go down with her. A twenty-five-year-old jockey, Robert Pineda, was killed in the spill and two others were seriously injured. Although no hard evidence has ever linked Bute directly to breakdowns, it is widely believed that rest, which would allow inflamed joints to heal, would be preferable to Bute, which simply reduces the soreness enough so that joints can continue to be stressed.

Lasix, on the other hand, has been used about as frequently today in racing as condoms at the Mustang Ranch in Las Vegas, Nevada. The "no glove no love" use of Lasix, however, appears to be on the decline among a number of trainers.

Since medications appear to be part of racing for the foreseeable future, it would be wise for any handicapper to look carefully at the impact these drugs have on the performance of a given horse. In writing this book, I have gone back myself and traced the performances over the past year of 100 horses on Lasix from their first published usage of the drug, and I have found no real track record of enhanced performances.

♣ **LEADING TRAINERS**

Gerald S. Bennett
Lynne Scace
Barbara McBride
Kirk Zaide
Jane Cibelli
Thomas Proctor
Ronald Allen

I have found instances in places like Florida and California, however, where horses on Lasix tend to perform worse on very hot and humid days. But when they are returned to cooler climates, they tend to return to form.

Florida is known for its sameness. As you can see, during winter racing, some of the very same trainers that you have followed during the spring, summer, and fall continue to appear at certain tracks like Tampa Bay. It should also be noted that there are two other trainers who, when they "get on a roll," have an extraordinary record of consistently finishing in the money. These trainers are Charley Fontana and Barbara McBride.

By this point, I think I have beaten you to death with my top four points, which include: know your track, trainers, and jockeys. And, like any form of analysis, you must have the necessary tools. Having now seen trainers move to Florida for the winter, you will see how you can get an edge on the spring meetings at Finger Lakes, Great Lakes, and Lone Star.

Tampa Bay Downs has had the largest collection of female jockeys at one time. One of the most successful came on February 12, 1981, when Julie Krone, then an apprentice, won her first race aboard Lord Farkle for trainer Les St. Leon. Carrying on in her footsteps is Tammi Piemarini.

But the hottest duo is trainer Gerald Bennett and jockey Daniel Centeno; those who have a wise eye would key in their races. Not to be outdone is the trio who graduated from the Laffitt Pincay Riding School in Panama—Jose Lezcano, Eddie Castro, and Fernando Guera. While the three jockeys do not resemble each other off a horse, their riding styles seem to mirror each other in the saddle. The only real intangible difference between the three is that Jose Lezcano has a 43 percent winning record with horses who have added blinkers, while the other two muster 17 percent and 14 percent respectively.

♣ LEADING JOCKEYS

Daniel Centeno

Jose Lezcano

Carlos Montalvo

Luis Antonio Gonzalez

Vernon Bush

Jose Ferrer

Pedro xLuis Cotto

Jose Martinez

Tammi Piemarini

There are times when both the betting public and the track become overly influenced by owners, trainers, and jockeys. This frequently applies in maiden races, as in the February 2 race card. Smoke Shop came into the race with only one prior start and that was at seven furlongs. In looking at the chart of the race, Smoke Shop made one move mid-race, but tailed off to finish fourth behind three closers in what can only be called a moderate time.

Conversely, when you look at Gemway, you see a horse that has had more experience at a variety of distances. Although still a maiden, she had finished in the money in three of the last seven starts. Also, a close look at Gemway shows that this horse tends to improve when racing at a distance over an "off" track. Finally, Gemway has champion bloodlines of both Conquistador Ciello and Cox's Ridge.

The second horse that I looked at in this race was City Thriller, who has had five prior starts, all of which were in higher-class races. This drop-down in class, combined with the fact that the horse had raced at this distance before, meant she finished third.

The third selection for this race was Steel Breeze. Although he had only one start and showed bullet workouts, add the fact that he was being ridden by a jockey who was one of the leaders, and he finished in the money during this meet.

The final selection for this race was Likethatonlybeta, whose numbers equate to the third selection.

Therefore, the final betting selections for this race were exacta, trifecta 2-4-6-7 box, and daily doubles 6-4, 6-1, 6-2.

♣ TAMPA BAY DOWNS, FEBRUARY 2, 2007—1ST RACE

MAIDEN CLAIMING - Six And One-Half Furlongs/Claiming Price $12,500
Purse: $10,000.

PN	ENTRY	JOCKEY	WEIGHT	MED.
1	Smoke Shop	Rocco, Jr., Joseph	120	L
2	Likethatonlybeta	Amiss, David	120	L
3	Zephyr Up	Piermarini, Tammi	120	
4	Steel Breeze	Garcia, Jesse	120	L
5	Brilliant Reason	Gilberto, Laiz	120	
6	Gemway	Cotto, Jr., Pedro	120	L
7	City Thriller	Centeno, Daniel	120	L
8	El Revelde	Fernandes, Braulio	120	

PN	ENTRY	SPEED	CLASS	DISTANCE	STYLE	INTANGIBLES	TOTAL
1	Smoke Shop	10	8	2	3	0	23
2	Likethatonlybeta	6	9	9	7	2	33
3	Zephyr Up	9	7	5	6	0	27
4	Steel Breeze	4	6	6	8	1	25
5	Brilliant Reason	5	5	7	4	0	21
6	Gemway	10	10	8	9	5	42
7	City Thriller	8	4	4	5	0	21
8	El Revelde	3	3	3	2	0	11

PN	ENTRY	WIN	PLACE	SHOW
6	Gemway	8.80	4.60	4.00
2	Likethatonlybeta		4.00	3.00
4	Steel Breeze			8.00

EXACTA	26.20	TRIFECTA	314.80

The second race again proved that speed in sprint races is not the end-all and be-all in determining race results. The analysis of the field of six once again eliminated Rowdy's A Warrior, the morning line favorite, and second choice Blues Fever. While it is true that both horses had broken their maiden in their last prior starts, both horses had significant negatives that decreased their potential in finishing in the money in the field of six. By the way, Rowdy's A Warrior had been claimed after his last race for $12,000.

♣ TAMPA BAY DOWNS, FEBRUARY 2, 2007—RACE 2

CLAIMING - Three-Year-Olds which have never won three races/Claiming Price: $10,300/Six Furlongs/Purse:

PN	ENTRY	JOCKEY	WEIGHT	MED.
1	I Can't Dance	Piermarini, Tammi	122	L
2	You'remakingmemad	Montalvo, Carlos	118	L
3	Joseph G	Bush, Vernon	118	L
4	Line Euro	Amiss, David	118	L
5	Rowdy's A Warrior	Yang, Chin	122	L
6	Blues Fever	Cosme, Emanuel	118	L

PN	ENTRY	SPEED	CLASS	DISTANCE	STYLE	INTANGIBLES	TOTAL
1	I Can't Dance	10	9	7	8		34
2	You'remakingmemad	10	8	10	9		37
3	Joseph G	8	10	4	10		32
4	Line Euro	9	6	7	8	+5	35
5	Rowdy's A Warrior	7	6	9	6		28
6	Blues Fever	6	6	6	7		25

PN	ENTRY	WIN	PLACE	SHOW
4	Line Euro	13.20	7.40	3.60
1	I Can't Dance		12.60	4.40
2	You'remakingmemad			3.20

EXACTA	126.40	TRIFECTA	455.20

When I first looked at the fourth race there were thirteen entrants. Normally, I hate races with that many horses because I know that for a place like Tampa Bay, the final starting horses will be around ten. But when I looked down the chart, I saw a jockey that I recognized from Suffolk Downs in Boston, Chantal Southerland. She was riding a John Kimmel filly named With Affirmation. On paper, she looked slower than Methuselah, but her class seemed to jump off the paper. She was a progeny of With Approval and Affirmed bloodlines. She had spent the last year racing at Belmont and Gulfstream on the dirt. One look at her feet and you could see that she was a turf horse. The second horse that I looked at was Royal Sip. She was a Jonathan Shepard shipper from Delaware Park. The big question I had was that although she had had success at Delaware on the turf, she had been laid up since September 2006. Five months without a race seemed too much to overlook, so I took a pass. The other two horses that I looked at were Mabel Syrup, who appeared to find her appropriate class and was ridden by jockey Richard Monterrey, who would probably carry this horse the last one-sixteenth to finish in the money, and I'm Raven, who had recently changed trainers from Harry Benson to Norman Pointer. With jockey Pedro Cotto aboard, I'm Raven both seemed to have had success on the turf. So my investment was to box 3-7-9 in the exacta and the trifecta.

♣ TAMPA BAY DOWNS, FEBRUARY 2, 2007—RACE 4

MAIDEN CLAIMING –Fillies and Mares Four Years old And Up/(Turf)-Mile and 1/16th Purse: $15,000.

PN	ENTRY	JOCKEY	WEIGHT	MED.
1	Risky Dreamer	Escobar, Martin	120	
2	Like A Saint	Garcia, Jesse	116	L
3	Mabel Syrup	Monterrey, Richard	120	L
4	Lear's Ruby	Cosme, Emanuel	116	L
5	Royal Sip	Jurado, Enrique	116	L
6	Lover	Montalvo, Carlos	120	L
7	With Affirmation	Sutherland, Chantal	120	L
8	Molly's Event	Gonzalez, Luis	120	L
9	I'm Raven	Cotto, Jr., Luis	120	L

PN	ENTRY	SPEED	CLASS	DISTANCE	STYLE	INTANGIBLES	TOTAL
1	Risky Dreamer	8	5	6	7		26
2	Like A Saint	9	4	7	7		22
3	Mabel Syrup	2	8	8	8	+4	30
4	Lear's Ruby	4	10	9	6		29
5	Royal Sip	1	9	9	6		25
6	Lover	7	6	6	5		24
7	With Affirmation	1	10	9	9	+5	34
8	Molly's Event	5	6	6	6		23
9	I'm Raven	3	10	10	10		33

PN	ENTRY	WIN	PLACE	SHOW
7	With Affirmation	3.80	3.20	2.40
9	I'm Raven		6.00	3.40
3	Mabel Syrup			3.80

EXACTA	25.2O	TRIFECTA	173.00

Success in wagering is the ability to perform consistently, and I returned four days later to again make sure that I was on top of Tampa Bay. With that in mind, let's look at the third race on February 6th. It was a 6½-furlong maiden-claiming race for three-year-olds with a purse of $8,000. There was a field of twelve.

The form handicap showed 3-6-5-8. As far as Montcalm Street and AP Speedway, I may have agreed with them; but as far as Andiamo Amico and Hothersal Turning, I believed that both should be eliminated from consideration in anything other than a superfecta.

♣ TAMPA BAY DOWNS, FEBRUARY 6, 2007—RACE 3

MAIDEN CLAIMING - For Three Year Olds and Upward/Fillies and Mares (NWI 6M)/Claiming Price: $8,000/Six and One-Half Furlongs On The Dirt/Purse: $8,100.

PN	ENTRY	JOCKEY	WEIGHT	MED.
1	Super Partner	Rosendo, Irwin	120	L b
2	Playin for Money	Daigle, Eric	120	L
3	Montcalm Street	Centeno, Daniel	120	L bf
4	Merton's Heart	Troxell, Kristin	113	L
5	A P Speedway	Oliveira, Polliana	112	L
6	Andiamo Amico	Martinez, Jr., Jose	120	L b
7	Devil's Playground	Faine, Craig	120	L
8	Hothersal Turning	Lezcano, Jose	120	L
9	St. Simon's Love	Garcia, Jesse	120	bf
10	Bookend	Cedeno, Lizetta	120	L b
11	Sins Are Forgiven	Foley, Tom	120	
12	Hard Ten	Gonzalez, Luis	120	L

PN	ENTRY	SPEED	CLASS	DISTANCE	STYLE	INTANGIBLES	TOTAL
1	Super Partner	7	6	7	6	7	33
2	Playin for Money	5	5	5	5	5	25
3	Montcalm Street	9	8	9	8	9	43
4	Merton's Heart	6	6	6	6		24
5	A P Speedway	8	7	8	7	9	39
6	Andiamo Amico	7	7	7	7	7	35
7	Devil's Playground	4	4	4	4	4	20
8	Hothersal Turning	5	6	6	6	6	30
9	St. Simon's Love	4	5	6	5	4	24
10	Bookend	5	6	5	5	4	24
11	Sins Are Forgiven	6	3	3	3	3	18
12	Hard Ten	4	2	2	2	2	12

PN	ENTRY	WIN	PLACE	SHOW
3	Montcalm Street	5.80	3.80	3.20
5	A P Speedway		5.60	4.20
1	Super Partner			4.40

EXACTA	33.00	TRIFECTA	90.60

Joe Calascribetta, Nick Zito, and Ronnie Beherns are three of the most successful trainers. While all three may have started with $8,000 claimers, they are in the race solely for either work or for sale. Remember what I said about knowing your trainers and jockeys. In this case, Zito got away with a 112-pound apprentice J. Oliveira aboard a speed burner that paid $5.60 for Place money and a $33.00 exacta. As for Andiamo Amico, he stumbled out of the gate like he had taken a three-way cold tablet and was moving in three directions at the same time. But Hothersal Turning seemed to just spit the bit and called it a day.

I said to you earlier that I tried to stay away from betting the first two races, but here is an example where I found something in the second race at Tampa.

♣ TAMPA BAY DOWNS, FEBRUARY 8, 2007—RACE 2

CLAIMING — For 4 Year Olds and Up-Fillies and Mares/Claiming Price: $16,000 - $15,000/ Six Furlongs On The Dirt/Purse: $16,200.

PN	ENTRY	JOCKEY	WEIGHT	MED.
1	Debere	Ferrer, Jose	118	L b
2	Simply Fancy	Rosario, Yamil	118	L bf
3	Mary Swan	Centeno, Daniel	118	L
4	Taupo	Montalvo, Carlos	120	L
5	We Will Dance	Jurado, Enrique	122	L b
6	Straight Glitter	Gonzalez, Luis	118	L

PN	ENTRY	SPEED	CLASS	DISTANCE	STYLE	INTANGIBLES	TOTAL
1	Debere	9	6	7	8		30
2	Simply Fancy	7	7	5	5		24
3	Mary Swan	6	9	6	6		27
4	Taupo	10	8	7	8		33
5	We Will Dance	8	10	9	10		37
6	Straight Glitter	5	5	8	8		26

PN	ENTRY	WIN	PLACE	SHOW
4	Taupo	10.00	5.00	3.40
2	Simply Fancy		9.80	4.40
5	We Will Dance			3.00

EXACTA	64.60	TRIFECTA	225.00

Whether you chose to look at the Beyers speed ratings or just the times of his last three six-furlong races, Taupo, who was a shipper from Hoosier Downs, was the speed of the race. Trainer Barbara McBride has had a history of success at six-furlong races at this track. Add to that the fact that the jockey had already won on this mount at the same distance fifteen days prior. In addition, Taupo beat Mary Swan on what was called a wet-fast track.

My second choice for this race was Simply Fancy. This horse was claimed out of a $16,000 Delaware Claiming race and then was claimed again when he was shipped to Tampa. But the key was the fact that this horse had won against $20,000 claimers. Plus, remember what I said about hot jockeys? Jockey Yamil Rosario had been on a roll, finishing in the money nearly 54 percent over the past several weeks. My third choice was We Will Dance. Trainer Steven Standridge got this six-furlongs specialist from Keith York, who is known around the Kentucky circuit for speed racers. Looking down the form, you can see that this horse had been placed in a $50,000 Claiming race at Keeneland. The exacta paid $64.60 and the trifecta paid $225.00.

In the fourth race on the same card, I found a true challenge. The race was a $13,500 Maiden Claiming race on the turf going one and one-sixteenth miles.

♣ TAMPA BAY DOWNS, FEBRUARY 8, 2007—RACE 4

MAIDEN CLAIMING –Four Years Olds and Upward/Claiming Price: $50,000-$45,000/
One and One Sixteenth Miles On The Turf/Purse: $15,000.

PN	ENTRY	JOCKEY	WEIGHT	MED.
1	Darned Bird	Winnett, Jr., Buddy	120	L b
3	Growing Wild	Lezcano, Jose	116	L
5	Deerstalker	Forest, Charles	120	L b
6	Ecru Egret	Cotto, Jr., Pedro	120	L b
7	Silver Heist	Gonzalez, Luis	120	L
8	Kriss Me Once	Bush, Vernon	120	L
9	Americanism	Centeno, Daniel	120	L b

PN	ENTRY	SPEED	CLASS	DISTANCE	STYLE	INTANGIBLES	TOTAL
1	Darned Bird	5	1				L
3	Growing Wild	4	2				L
5	Deerstalker	6	3				L
6	Ecru Egret	10	10				L
7	Silver Heist	4	4				L
8	Kriss Me Once	6	6				L
9	Americanism	8	8				L

PN	ENTRY	WIN	PLACE	SHOW
3	Growing Wild	18.80	9.00	4.80
9	Americanism		4.60	3.00
8	Kriss Me Once			5.00

EXACTA	78.60	TRIFECTA	412.80

You have probably noticed that up to this point that I have concentrated on races held on the dirt. This has been because most of the tracks that I have reviewed only have dirt tracks. But there also are some differences in the analysis of turf racing.

The first difference is that turf racing has a completely different set of track standards than flat or dirt racing. There are five classifications of turf conditions:

Firm
Is similar to that of a fast dirt classification. It has a thick cushion and is slightly springy.

Hard
Is when blazing sun has thinned out the grass, similar to what happens to home lawns.

Yielding
Is when the soil is soft enough that it seems to have no spring.

Soft
Is when the turf is so wet that the horse sinks into it, just like they do on a muddy dirt track.

Good
Is a consistentcy that is harder then Yielding but still has some pliability.

Most European horses that come to America prefer Yielding, Soft, or Good turf because it is similar to what they race upon at home. But most American courses tend to like Firm or Hard. Despite the frequent showers of southern Florida, the courses primarily range from Firm to Hard, while courses from New York to Kentucky tend to be Yielding.

The second difference is in the analysis of the past performances. Because early speed is not as important as position, particular attention should be paid to horses coming from off-the-pace as well as final furlong time.

Thirdly, don't assume that a good dirt jockey is also a good turf rider. The same logic should be used when looking at a good speed rider as opposed to a steeplechase rider. Here's an analogy: Shaquille O'Neal is a center—you don't expect him to play guard.

Having achieved my profit for the day, I decided to try betting against the form on a turf race at Tampa. While I, primarily, can call myself a form player, there are occasions when the camera turns to the paddock area and what you see tends to be way off from what's on the form. Or what you see starts to point you back to your notes.

This was the case when I tore up my analysis and called an audible at the last minute. Growing Wild, who I had seen in her last outing at Calder on November 25, looked like a dead man walking. In fact, when I went back to my racing program of that day, I looked at my notes of the race. I wrote in the margin, "Growing Wild looked about as comfortable on dirt as a Snickers bar in a swimming pool. Should try on the turf. Look at her feet." As I looked at this horse in the paddock area, she looked like a "live" horse. She was up on her toes and appeared ready for action. Also, she had two other things in her favor—jockey Jose Lezcano and weight: she was to carry only 116 pounds.

A horse that in her past two starts seemed to be out for an exercise excursion, this time she looked like she came to run. Her $18.80 Win price proved that fact. Since I combined her in a box with Americanism and Kiss Me Once in both the exacta ($78.60) and the trifecta ($412.80), my investment resulted in a $245.70 profit.

So you see that by knowing your track, having knowledge of the trainers and jockeys, having the analytical tools necessary, placing your bet either online or by phone, and limiting your downside risk by selectively placing bets on no more than five races at any given track, you've increased your odds for success. You can further advance your probability of success by choosing exotic wagering in order to maximize your investment and look for a realistic rate of return.

Also, the realistic analysis of speed, class, distance, and style are usually the most important intangibles. In this instance, the intangibles were the horse itself. Sure, it might have been implied by the morning odds of 5-1, but a straight analysis of the past performances pushed the betting public to ignore the fact that the horse had a turf pedigree both on his father's and mother's side.

It's times like these when I refer to the saying of an old friend who tipped me off to a turf horse by the name of Wajima. He said, "Man, the horse has more grass in his pedigree than a Rastafarian."

The fifth race of the day reminded me of a topic that I had forgotten to include—Inquiry.

There is no more painful feeling than slaving over a racing form and picking out a winner, only to lose based upon a disqualification. So let's talk about *policing* the race.

While the placing judges determine the order in which the horses have crossed the finish line, they aren't the ones that make the results "official." That responsibility rests with the track's three stewards, who are the track's most senior racing officials. The "official" sign is lit only when the stewards have determined that no violations of racing rules have taken place during the course of the race.

In the early days of racing, the most common racing rule was "every man for himself." Rough riding was the rule rather than the exception; cutting off or slamming into other horses was another everyday occurrence. Racing officials were appointed to their positions not because of their racing knowledge, but because of their prominence in the community. Their rulings tended to be restricted to placing horses at the finish line.

When the Jockey Club was formed to provide central administration for the then chaotic sport of racing, the members formulated racing rules that included prohibitions of rough riding and other dangerous race tactics. Enforcing them, however, still depended on how keenly developed the powers of perception of the racing officials were, and on how skillful they were in interpreting racing law. With only their eyes and memories to guide them, many violations were missed and many violators went unpunished.

The solution came with the institution of the film patrol. While to this day, professional football, baseball, and basketball resist using slow-motion cameras as a backup for the judgment of their officials, racing has used this sophisticated technique since after World War II. Today, at least four different cameras, placed on towers around the racetrack, record each race.

As good as tapes and films are, however, they have to be interpreted. Racing still depends on the skill of its racing officials. In the 1930s, the Jockey Club formed its "School for Racing Officials." This rigorous training program is a prerequisite for obtaining a job as an official at most tracks today. Every race is reviewed by at least seven officials. Four or more patrol judges are stationed at the three critical points around the track—at the start, at the turns, and at the finish line.

These patrol judges are in constant communication with the three stewards, who sit in the stewards' booth high above the track. In front of the stewards are at least four television sets that show the race as seen by each of the four or more cameras. The stewards also watch the race through binoculars.

What the patrol judges and stewards are watching for are violations considered in light of the Rules of Racing, which are listed below:

Rule 153

(a) When clear, a horse may be taken to any part of the course provided that crossing or weaving in front of contenders may not constitute interference or intimidation for which the offender may be disciplined.

(b) A horse crossing another so as to actually to impede him is disqualified, unless the impeded horse was partly at fault or the crossing was wholly caused by the fault of some other horse or jockey.

(c) If a horse or jockey jostles another horse, the aggressor may be disqualified, unless the impeded horse or his jockey was partly at fault or the jostle was wholly caused by the fault of some other horse or jockey.

(d) If a jockey willfully strikes another horse or jockey, or rides willfully or carelessly so as to cause other horses to do so, his horse is disqualified.

Note that in the above rules, no mention is made of winning. Whether or not the foul was flagrant enough to keep a horse from winning is not part of the decision to disqualify. Actual contact is also not necessary for a foul—only that the horse be "impeded" or caused to alter its course.

If the placing judges or the stewards notice any suspicious incidents in the course of the race, the stewards may delay the posting of the official results for a steward's inquiry. Even if no inquiry is posted by the stewards, any trainer or jockey may lodge an objection, which causes the stewards to conduct an inquiry.

The stewards follow a two-step procedure during an inquiry or objection. First, they talk by telephone to the riders involved—first to the rider of the horse allegedly interfered with, then to the rider of the alleged offender. They then carefully replay tapes of the incident from all available cameras, going over them as many times as needed before making a decision.

Until the last three decades, horses that were disqualified were placed last. Under the present rules of racing, however, if the stewards decide to disqualify, the offending horse is placed back only as far as needed to place it behind the injured party. Thus, a winner who is disqualified for interfering with the third-place horse is placed third; the second finisher becomes the winner and the third finisher becomes the Place horse. To discourage time-consuming frivolous claims, the stewards have the authority to fine the jockey or trainer making such a claim.

The morning after a horse is disqualified, the stewards meet again with the offending jockey to determine if the incident took place because of the rider's careless or dangerous riding. If they decide the jockey is at fault, a suspension is ordered. The most common suspension periods are three or seven days.

Even if no inquiry or objection is lodged for a race, the stewards need one more signal before the race is pronounced "official." After a race, each rider dismounts and then is weighed out under the supervision of the Clerk of Scales or his assistant. After allowance is made for mud picked up on wet days, the weight is checked off against the pre-race weight. If all is in order, the Clerk of Scales picks up a telephone and notifies the stewards. At this point, the race is pronounced official. Once displayed "official," prices are posted and the public moves to the windows to collect their winnings and place their bets for the next race.

Next, there is an occurrence that has happened to me twice. I'm talking about betting on a horse, having him lose, then finding out weeks later that the winner had failed a drug test. Where does the bettor stand? The horse I bet on, which came in second, could have been the winner!

I find no satisfaction in the statement that the public gets paid when the "official" sign is posted; the owners have to wait for their purses. After every race, the winner, the second-place finisher, the beaten favorite, and any other horses designated by the stewards proceed directly to the drug-testing barn (known around the track as the "spit barn"). In that barn, blood and urine samples are taken and labeled, then shipped to a drug-testing laboratory. If a horse, as sometimes happens, refuses to cooperate immediately with a urine sample, the animal has to stay in the barn under guard until the sample is obtained or for a specified number of hours.

The incredible variety of pharmaceutical substances and the constant appearance of new products make drug testing incredibly complicated. Presently, laboratories routinely conduct tests for nearly a hundred different substances. If any drugs have been found by racing security at the track involved, additional tests for those substances may be taken. This drug testing, depending on the state, can take from five to fifteen days.

If the drug reports are negative, the stewards order the release of the purse money to the owner. If they test positive, the horse is disqualified to last place and the purses are ordered and distributed in the new order of finish. The most famous such redistribution was the disqualification of Dancer's Image in the 1968 Kentucky Derby. The horse, owned by Peter Fuller, was found to have traces of Butazolidin, an anti-inflammatory drug which, ironically, was later legalized for use on horses in Kentucky; it is now still banned in the state of Kentucky though.

As of 1980, pre-race drug testing was introduced at New York tracks in a further effort to protect the betting public.

While all of that is fine and good, I still lost money. Again, I repeat—where does the bettor stand? The horse I bet on, which came in second, could have been the winner!

CHAPTER SEVEN

Turfway Park

ONE OF THE things that happens when deciding to replace a track is you forget about tracks that you used to play on a "hit and miss" basis. These are tracks that you have played occasionally during the winter months when one of your regular tracks is dark or the weather has caused a cancellation. One of these tracks is Turfway Park.

Turfway Park in Florence, Kentucky, would not be considered a major-league racetrack, mostly because it must compete for prime racing dates in Kentucky with such super-heavyweights as Churchill Downs and Keeneland Race Course. And if the other two had their say, Turfway might never be a major-league racetrack. But for one afternoon every fall, it does put on one heck of a big-time show.

Turfway also shows up those who believe the myth that stake winners never come to smaller tracks. Back in 2000, Kentucky Cup Championship Day was renewed for the seventh straight year on September 15 at Turfway. The six previous editions had made enough noise nationally to earn graded status for four of the six Kentucky Cup Championship races. Both the $500,000 Kentucky Cup Classic for three-year-olds and upward at a mile and an eighth and the $150,000 Kentucky Cup Sprint for three-year-olds at six furlongs became Grade II races. The $250,000 Turfway Breeders' Cup for fillies and mares at a mile and a sixteenth, and the $100,000 Kentucky Cup Juvenile for two-year-olds at a mile and a sixteenth each became Grade III events. Other stakes that have run continually since the first Kentucky Cup Day in 1994 are the One Mile $100,000 KC Juvenile Fillies and the $50,000 Inexcessivelygood Starter Handicap—also at a mile; this last race is named in honor of a Bob Baffert trainee who broke down during the stretch drive of the Jim Beam Stake at Turfway in 1997.

The Kentucky Cup is what's commonly known in the sport as a "Blue Plate Special" or a "showcase day," meaning that a track puts on a series of stake races during an afternoon, as opposed to a single "black type event," among Allowance, Maiden, and Claiming offerings. Inspired by the first Breeders' Cup Championship Day in 1984, ABC Television broadcaster and Maryland horseman Jim McKay initiated the idea of showcase days at a local level. McKay was the main force in putting together the first Maryland Million Day in 1986—it is a card loaded with stake races for Maryland-sired Thoroughbreds. The Maryland Million has spawned many imitations; there are more than twenty such showcase days that are run annually on the American racing calendar.

Like the Maryland Million, nearly every showcase day has at least one race for either state-breds—horses that are sired by a stallion standing in the state, or horses that are stabled regularly at the host track. The idea, of course, is to highlight not only the best of local racing talent, but to showcase the state's breeding program.

The Kentucky Cup, however, offers no such restrictions for their six stake races. It might seem a touch redundant if they did. Kentucky-breds comprise more than 40 percent of the annual American foal crop and generally are considered to have the best pedigrees in this country. As a consequence, Turfway officials were not burdened with the millstone of having to put on an all-day racing commercial for the Kentucky breeding program and instead were free to open their races to all comers. One reason for the quick ascension of Kentucky Cup races is because of no restrictions. They have had a quick ascension not only in the ranks of showcase days, but also as a red-letter day on the American racing calendar.

The first Kentucky Cup Championship Day was conducted under the Turfway reign of Jerry Carroll. A Tennessee native, Carroll, along with partners, purchased in 1986 what was then Latonia Race Course for $13.5 million. Carroll changed the name to the more up-tempo Turfway Park and began making additional bold strokes to heighten the value of the northern Kentucky oval. Carroll and partners put millions of dollars into the renovation of the northern Kentucky plant. The track's marquee race, the $350,000 Jim Beam Stake, received a purse boost of $150,000. After 1987, it was increased in length from a mile and a sixteenth to a mile and an eighth, the distance of most key Kentucky Derby prep races. Carroll also was at the helm when pick three wagering made its Turfway debut in the fall of 1987. The following year, Turfway inaugurated inter-track wagering in Kentucky by simulcasting an entire card of races to patrons at Ellis Park in the southwestern part of the state.

Turfway also began to earn a reputation as a racetrack that could attract racehorses of national quality. Alysheba, "the pony from Latonie," broke his maiden at Turfway in the fall of 1986, then finished second in the track's In Memoriam Stake, a two-year-old race that also received a significant purse boost during Carroll's tenure. Alysheba, of course, went on to win the Kentucky Derby and Preakness Stake as a three-year-old, as well as the Breeders' Cup Classic at age four. When he retired, Alysheba was the leading money-winning horse of all time. In 1989 Kentucky Derby heroine Winning Colors won the Turfway Budweiser Breeders' Cup in what was to be the last stake win of her career.

The Jim Beam Stake also was blossoming into a race with national implications. In 1990 Summer Squall became the first Beam winner to win a classic. After finishing second in the Kentucky Derby to Unbridled, Summer Squall avenged that loss with a career effort in the Preakness. He began a remarkable four-year run of Beam winners who went on to become classic heroes. In 1991 it was Hansel powering to a Beam win in track-record time, then going on to take both the Preakness and Belmont. Lil E. Tee became the first Beam winner to take the grandest of all prizes—the Kentucky Derby—the following year. Prairie Bayou, an unsung gelding, swept to victory in both the Jim Beam and Preakness stakes in 1993.

Prior to Turfway's run of famous Jim Beam winners, the racetrack did not enjoy a stellar reputation with national horsemen. Turfway conducts a long meeting during the dead of winter. It's a part of the world that usually sees its fair share of freezing temperatures and snowstorms. Consequently, the track's racing surface could be volatile. If you had a speed horse racing over a track labeled frozen, you might make the rent. Otherwise, it would be a winter filled with bologna and cheese sandwiches. If you had a particularly fine-boned animal entered when the track was thawing, you'd be wise to keep that horse in the barn.

The oval's idiosyncratic nature gave it a reputation as one that could be brutal on shippers. The first Jim Beam Stake, run in 1983, reiterated the unfriendly host tag: nine entries arrived from out of town—they came from Aqueduct, Oaklawn, Fair Grounds, Hialeah, and Santa Anita—yet it was a totally obscure local-yokel named Good N' Dusty who won the race by five lengths at odds of 39-1.

Both Summer Squall and Hansel won races after spending the winter in Florida. Lil E. Tee arrived from Oaklawn, and Prairie Bayou arrived from Aqueduct. Each of these four runners earned a special place in the history at the northern Kentucky track for helping obliterate the notion that you had to stable at Turfway to win there. In fact, in the early 1990s, it seemed possible that you might be able to leave Turfway with a better horse than the one you had brought in.

While the Jim Beam brought fame to Turfway in the first half of the last decade, the track lacked a prominent race for its shortfall meet in September. The opportunity for good racing was there, though; stables from New York and Chicago arrived early in Kentucky to prepare for the difficult October meeting at Keeneland. Perhaps inspired mainly by its string of Beam winners, Turfway officials announced the inaugural Kentucky Cup Championship Day for the fall of 1994. The $400,000 Classic was the keynote event on the day's card; an overall $1 million in purse money was being offered on a single afternoon of racing at Turfway.

Both equine and human royalty showed up. Jockey Chris McCarron and eventual Sovereign Award–winner Pennyhill Park won the Turfway Breeders' Cup; Jerry Bailey booted home budding star Tejano Run in the KC Juvenile.

The main event, the Classic, brought together a breathtaking match between three-year-old Tabasco Cat, a D. Wayne Lukas trainee, who had won both the Preakness and Belmont Stakes during the summer, and California-based powerhouse Best Pal, a six-year-old multimillionaire still capable of a brilliant race. Youth was served as Tabasco Cat raced to a two-length win in 1994 over longshot Mighty Avanti. Best Pal did not fire his best and was third. Both Best Pal and Tabasco Cat did start in the Breeders' Cup Classic at Churchill Downs later that fall. Best Pal was unplaced, but

Tabasco Cat ran gamely and was beaten in a photo finish by the frantic stretch-runner Concern.

If Tabasco Cat provided the quick-dry cement to the foundation of KC Championship Day, Lukas has been the major post-and-beam man in building the Kentucky Cup into a prime-time event in the sport of Thoroughbred racing. Lukas has been a major player in each of the previous six Kentucky Cup Championships. Since 1994, he's won each KC race at least once, except for the Inexcessivelygood Handicap. His ten Kentucky Cup victories dwarf those of competing trainers (Bob Baffert, Robert Holthus, John Kimmel, Kenny McPeek, and Nick Zito, who were next with two wins apiece). In 1995, Lukas brought his own version of "Murderer's Row" to Turfway, winning four KC races with Thunder Gulch (Classic), Editor's Note (Juvenile), Lord Carson (Sprint), and Tipically Irish (Juvenile Fillies). He finished second in the Turfway Breeders' Cup with Serena's Song.

Thunder Gulch and Serena's Song were particularly notable catches for Turfway. Thunder Gulch had put together what was arguably the best three-year-old campaign of the decade, winning both the Kentucky Derby and the Belmont Stakes, as well as the Travers, Swaps, Florida Derby, and Fountain of Youth. He was in the twilight of that rugged season by the time he reached northern Kentucky. The Lukas colt struggled a bit to win the Classic over the hard-hitting local runner Judge T C in what proved to be the second last-start of Thunder Gulch's career.

Serena's Song, also a three-year-old of '95, already had become the first filly to win the Jim Beam Stake earlier that spring. Perhaps facing the best Beam field ever, she defeated Tejano Run and Mecke, earning herself a start in the Kentucky Derby. A runner who seemingly thrived on the demands of a Lukas campaign, Serena's Song failed in the Derby, but rebounded to take the L Black-Eyed Susan, the Mother Goose Stake, and the Haskell Invitational (also males). She failed that fall in the Turfway BC, but eventually went on to become racing's all-time female money earner.

Thus far, the Kentucky Cup has been a stepping-stone for six Eclipse winners. Lukas has trained four of them: Thunder Gulch, Golden Attraction, Boston Harbor, and Serena's Song. A pair of other Eclipse honorees raced at Turfway in the 1998 version of the Kentucky Cup. They were Reraise, a gelded son of Danzatore, and Silver Charm.

Reraise destroyed a handful of rivals in the KC Sprint, winning by 12 lengths in the sparkling time of 1:08 2/5. He went on to take the Breeders' Cup Sprint at Churchill Downs in early November, a victory that earned him year-end Eclipse honors in the sprint division.

Turfway might have landed its ultimate trophy-catch the same year. Silver Charm, already a hero of the '97 Kentucky Derby and Preakness, as well as the memorable winner of the $4-million Dubai World Cup the following spring, started as the heavy favorite in the '98 KC Classic. Also entered was the Metropolitan Mile (Grade I) and the Carter Handicap (Grade I) champ Wild Rush.

Silver Charm turned in one of his heart-stopping stretch drives in the Classic, though Wild Rush was equal to the challenge. Literally. They hooked up as a team turning for home and stayed that way throughout the final three-sixteenths of a mile. The result—a dead-heat, the first in Kentucky Cup history. They finished 17 lengths in front of third-place finisher Acceptable, a multiple-stake winner in his own right that year. The final time of 1:47 2/5 for the mile and an eighth matched the mark of Atticus, the KC Classic winner of 1996.

For Silver Charm, the win was pivotal. He was coming off a terrible effort at Del Mar, finishing worse than second for the first time in his career. His reputation as well as his fighting spirit were in need of repair. After winning the Turfway race, the Florida-bred went on to take the Santa Anita's Goodwood Handicap rather easily over old pal Free House, then finished second in the Breeders' Cup Classic against a remarkable field, which included Awesome Again, Swain, Victory Gallop, Coronado's Quest, Skip Away, Gentlemen, and Running Stag. (Wild Rush did not start again until the Breeders' Cup Sprint, where he left the gate as a slight favorite against 13 rivals. He never got untracked that day, however, finishing well back of Reraise.)

That year also marked the last Kentucky Cup during the Carroll years. Turfway was sold in early winter '99 for $37 million to the Keeneland Association, Harrah's Casinos, and Dreamport (a division of G-Tech, a company that manufactures video lottery terminals). Carroll took his promotional skills to the rapidly growing sport of auto racing, developing a new speedway in northern Kentucky, which opened earlier this year. Keeneland's new partnership with a casino company and another that manufactured video lottery terminals left some industry insiders uneasy; but if there are to be any ill effects, Turfway and Kentucky Cup have yet to see them. In the fall of 1999, each Kentucky Cup race offered the same purse as the previous year. The KC Classic was rewarded with its first Breeders' Cup Classic winner when Cat Thief parlayed a third-place finish at Turfway into a startling upset later that fall at Gulfstream Park. The Kentucky Cup also saw a record live attendance last year when 10,807 patrons pushed through the turnstiles, an increase for the third consecutive year. The numbers for on-track and off-track handles were more puzzling. Turfway bettors pushed $1,292,062 through the windows, far below on-track numbers earlier in the decade. Total wagering on the Kentucky Cup races last year was reported as $7,165,004, a dramatic decrease from the all-time high of more than $9.5 million in 1997.

It's difficult to gauge whether or not the Kentucky Cup has already seen its best days. Though considered an outsider in the world of Thoroughbred racing, Carroll dutifully promoted the races and was fortunate enough to make the afternoon a red-letter one on the busy schedule of the most famous trainer in the sport—D. Wayne Lukas. If the Kentucky Cup survives well into the twenty-first century, both men deserve equal credit for having brought immediate prestige to these races. And while it is difficult to imagine Keeneland allowing any aspect of Kentucky racing to fall into disrepair, the venerable Lexington Association and its new partners have a hard act to follow. Thus far, the autumn sun in the bluegrass has shone brightly on Kentucky Cup Day.

Kentucky Cup races are not restricted to the main track at Turfway Park. Down I-65 a piece, actually about 200 miles, is the all-turf Kentucky Downs, located in Franklin, just north of the Tennessee border.

In conjunction with KC 2000, Kentucky Downs will be offering its own brand of Kentucky Cup on September 23, 2007. For the second consecutive year, the Franklin oval will card four stake races that will offer $700,000 in combined purse money. The black-type races kick-off with the $100,000 Kentucky Cup Turf Dash for three-year-olds and upward at six furlongs. Followed by the Ellen $100,000 Kentucky Cup Ladies Turf for three-year-olds and upward, fillies, and mares, at one mile; the $200,000 Kentucky Cup Mile for three-year-olds and upward, also at one mile; and the $300,000 Kentucky Cup Turf for three-year-olds and upward at a mile and a half.

Perhaps the best horse to step on the Kentucky Downs lawn last fall was Pleasant Temper, a multiple graded-stakes winning daughter of Storm Cat. Sent off as the odds-on favorite in the Ladies Turf, she went unchallenged throughout, posting a three-length victory under Pat Day. Pleasant Temper went on to start in the inaugural edition of Breeders' Cup Filly & Mare Turf last fall at Gulfstream Park, though she wound up unplaced in the big field of fourteen.

Treat Me Doc, Illinois bred, lit the tote board for a $65.80 mutuel in the KC Mile. Facing the proven middle distance runners Commitisize and Inkatha, Treat Me Doc and his rider, Jon Court, rated just behind a contentious pace, swung six wide in the lane, and got up in time to defeat Dernier Croise by a head.

A troika of Irish-breds stole the top spots in the '99 Kentucky Cup Turf. Fahris, owned by the powerful Shadwell Stable, nabbed pacesetter Yaqthan in the final yards of the mile-and-a-half tilt. Royal Strand, like Pleasant Temper (an Elliott Walden trainee), stalked the lead throughout and tired in the final 40 yards to wind up third. Kentucky Cup Turf events have yet to draw anywhere near the quality of fields enjoyed thus far at the Turfway races. The one-mile distance is certainly popular enough in this country; both KC Mile and KC Ladies Turf seem the most likely candidates this year to draw top Midwestern lawn specialists tuning up for Keeneland and/or a Breeders' Cup start.

There are two factors that might be working against Kentucky Cup Turf races thus far: (a) None of the races are graded as yet. (b) With its undulating ground and asymmetrically-shaped oval, the Kentucky Downs turf course more resembles something found in Europe than anything in the United States. While the differences are subtle, horsemen have been known to shy away from what is considered standard racing in that country.

But this is horse racing, friends, so you never know what kind of horse might surface somewhere near the Tennessee border this fall in preparation for the race of its life. The Franklin track has already caught lightning in a bottle once—-in 1994, an unheralded mare named One Dreamer parlayed a third-place finish in Dueling Grounds' Rachel Jackson Stake into a 47-1 shocker in the Breeders' Cup Distaff at Churchill Downs.

♣ LEADING TRAINERS

NAME	STARTS	FIRST	SECOND	THIRD	EARNINGS
Kim Hammond	60	12	14	4	$92,634
Paul McGee	33	9	6	4	$142,706
Elwood 0. McCann, Sr.	15	8	0	2	$62,063
0. Michael Smithwick, Jr	21	7	3	3	$105,422
Eddie Kenneally	21	6	6	5	$92,354
Helen Pitts	20	6	3	2	$63,907
Philip A. Sims	16	6	2	4	$103,326
Oscar Hall	19	6	1	1	$56,532
David P. England	35	5	7	6	$56,634
Dennis T. Moore	22	5	2	2	$28,049
Jeff Talley	10	5	2	1	$55,517
William R. Connelly	43	4	9	3	$72,045
S. Joe Cain	34	4	7	4	$58,267
Michael. Maker	25	4	7	2	$54,569
Dale I. Romans	39	4	4	9	$93,830
Vincent White	28	4	4	3	$47,056
Patrick L Biancone	21	4	4	1	$59,470
William Bradley	40	4	3	5	$85,041
Eric R. Reed	24	4	3	4	$66,546
Gregory D. Foley	42	4	2	8	$83,493

*Starting Date: 01/01/2007; Ending Date: 02/26/2007

♣ LEADING JOCKEYS

Name	Starts	1st	2nd	3rd	Earnings
Miguel Mena	230	46	37	27	$563,849
AlonsoQuinonez	243	44	34	38	$533,495
Julien R. Leparoux	188	43	37	24	$546,318
Victor Lebron	208	25	29	34	$324,123
Dean P. Butler	139	21	17	14	$217,731
Rodney A. Prescott	171	19	28	21	$279,974
Perry Wayne Ouzts	216	18	18	24	$190,676
Inosenclo Diego	143	16	17	9	$197,387
Orlando Mojica	103	16	16	23	$227,472

*Starting Date: 01/01/2007; Ending Date: 02/26/2007

♣ TURFWAY PARK, FEBRUARY 21, 2007—RACE 1

CLAIMING - Three-Year-Olds And Up/Fillies and Mares (NW3 L)/Claiming Price: $5,000/One Mile On The Dirt/Purse: $6,700.

PN	ENTRY	JOCKEY	WEIGHT	MED.
1	Evolutionary Lady (KY)	Schaefer, Gregory	120	L
2	Hurricane Hailey (ON)	Quinonez, Alonso	115	L b
3	Gone Gray (OH)	Butler, Dean	120	L b
4	Chiacchierone.(KY)	Ouzts, Perry	120	L b
5	Miss QuackerJack (KY)	Felix, Julio	120	L
6	Appealingtempting (KY)	Mena, Miguel	120	L b
7	Wakki Gold (KY)	Diego, Inosencio	120	L
8	Sleepwalker (KY)	Doser, Mary	124	L b

PN	ENTRY	SPEED	CLASS	DISTANCE	STYLE	INTANGIBLES	TOTAL
1	Evolutionary Lady (KY)	6	9	9	8		32
2	Hurricane Hailey (ON)	7	7	7	7		28
3	Gone Gray (OH)	10	6	5	5		26
4	Chiacchierone.(KY)	8	10	10	10		38
5	Miss QuackerJack (KY)	6	8	8	8		30
6	Appealingtempting (KY)	5	5	5	10		25
7	Wakki Gold (KY)	4	6	6	7		24
8	Sleepwalker (KY)	9	8	8	2		27

PN	ENTRY	WIN	PLACE	SHOW
4	Chiacchierone	3.60	2.40	2.40
2	Hurricane Hailey		3.60	3.00
1	Evolutionary Lady			4.60

EXACTA	17.20		TRIFECTA	80.40

The question in this race was: Did Hurricane Haley have enough stamina to go the distance of a mile? If not, Chiacchierone had been an off-the-pace runner who probably had given his owners, trainer, and bettors a heart attack trying to get the lead in the stretch. If both of them did fail, then look for either Evolutionary Lady or long-shot Gone Gray to pull off an upset. Of the two, I picked Evolutionary Lady. I don't think that Dean Butler and Gone Gray can steady this classic front-runner. My thoughts—a 1-2-4 exacta and a trifecta wager.

♣ TURFWAY PARK, FEBRUARY 21, 2007—RACE 2

MAIDEN CLAIMING – For Three Year Old Fillies/Claiming Price: $7,500
One Mile On The Dirt/Purse: $7,300.

PN	ENTRY	JOCKEY	WEIGHT	MED.
1	Fancy Gal	Troilo, William	122	L
2	Power Source	Ramirez, Emanuel	112	L
3	Benny's Girl	Felix, Julio	122	L
4	Blue Mistress	Diego, Inosencio	122	L b
5	Sapphire Lake	Camejo, Jose	122	Lb
6	Winin For Cathy	Enriquez, Juan	122	L
7	Secret Melody	Leparoux, Julien	122	L
8	Retirement Plus	Doser, Mary	122L b	
9	Carrie N Marcie	Coa, Daniel	122	L
10	Betcha I Can	Prescott, Rodney	122	L b

PN	ENTRY	SPEED	CLASS	DISTANCE	STYLE	INTANGIBLES	TOTAL
1	Fancy Gal	10	10	10	10		40
2	Power Source	4	10	10	10	+1	35
3	Benny's Girl	3	9	9	9		30
4	Blue Mistress	3	9	9	9		27
5	Sapphire Lake	8	5	5	5		23
6	Winin For Cathy	6	7	7	7		27
7	Secret Melody	6	6	6	6		24
8	Retirement Plus	2	4	4	4		14
9	Carrie N Marcie	2	3	3	3		11
10	Betcha I Can	6	7	7	7		27

PN	ENTRY	WIN	PLACE	SHOW
1	Fancy Gal	4.60	2.60	2.40
5	Sapphire Lake		3.60	3.80
7	Secret Melody			4.40

EXACTA	15.60	TRIFECTA	69.20

The second race was one of those situations where you realize that you should have taken a pass on the race because you know you're not going to really make any money out of it. Looking down the field, you have Fancy Gal, who is a prohibitive favorite. On paper, she looks so good that even a blind man could bet her. She's been the distance before; she's a front-runner with a come-catch-me determination. The second choice was Sapphire Lake, who comes from off the pace; and if the race was a mile and a sixteenth, there might be enough time. In her last three races, her real strength and speed seemed to have come from the second through the third quarter.

In situations like that, try to find a third horse that can make an investment worth your while. In that race, three horses all were within an eyelash of each other—Secret Melody, Betcha I Can, and Winin For Cathy. By the sheer numbers in that race with five horses in order to win a trifecta, the tip here is to just go on to the next race.

CHAPTER EIGHT

Summary

WHEN I WAS first asked about this book, the question that arose was, "Why are you using this caliber of track and not the 'majors' like Belmont, Saratoga, Woodbine, Laurel, Churchill Downs, Arlington, Santa Anita, and Del Mar?" My response was quite simple. They are not the roots.

In the first chapter I posed the question to you, "You Want the Money?" And I hope that in the past seven chapters, I've showed you that learning the trainers and the jockeys who perform at a given track will give you more insight into constructive betting. But there are instances when just analyzing from your living room rather than from the track will put you at a distinct disadvantage.

Thoroughbred racing is a sport filled with pageantry, lore, and action. If you listen to trainers, owners, and those with losing tickets, you will find that at least one mistake is made per race. But from each view of what the mistake may have been, at least from a wagering standpoint, you realize it is a thinking man and woman's game.

Handicapping is something that takes patience. In the end, you won't always be right, but you can learn to become better. But that's not to say that in the end there are times when your best bet may be the fact that you had to pass up a race. And in some instances, you'd end up just looking at the person next to you and asking his opinion or listening to the woman who says, "I just like the colors."

How to bet is determined by the results of one's handicapping. How much to bet, however, requires a separate set of judgments. One of the most common laments of the horseplayer is, "I'm a good handicapper but a lousy bettor."

While a handicapping ability is largely a matter of knowledge, successful betting depends on maintaining discipline under what can be emotional and pressure-laden situations. After carefully making his/her selections, a horseplayer notices a sudden, dramatic drop in the odds on another horse. In such cases, the urge to drop one's own selection and go with the "smart money" is overwhelming. Horseplayers find themselves ignoring horses going off at 3-1 to play long shots, or abandoning win betting to take a flyer on exactas and trifectas.

Even professional horseplayers find themselves succumbing to such pressures. A professional may go to the track to bet on only two races in which he has spotted sufficiently attractive overlays, but sitting out races is dull. For action, he may find himself placing a small wager or two. In the excitement, small bets grow larger. By the time the races he's been waiting for come up, the profit he's anticipated may still leave him a loser for the day.

Even more than the professional, the average race-goer enjoys having some money riding on every race. One solution is to bet the same amount on every race, be it $2 or $10; but, as we've explained in detail, some races are more playable than others. Logic suggests betting more money on some races than on others.

To solve this problem, some professionals divide their wagers into two kinds: "prime" bets and "action" bets. Prime bets are reserved for those overlays on which large profits depend. A professional may set a prime bet at 5 percent of his total betting capital. A typical racegoer who brings $50 to the track may decide to make three $10 prime bets during a day.

Action bets are the smaller wagers that provide entertainment between prime races. A professional may set an upper limit of $20 for action bets; the racing fan may divide the $20 left over after prime bets equally between the rest of the races on the card.

The distinction between prime bets and action bets is also useful in winning and losing streaks. Most experts advise bettors to increase betting during winning streaks, but the money should be added to prime bets; increasing action bets (because these bets are primarily for fun) will erode winnings in a hurry. In horseplaying, one encounters mystifying slumps when winners don't come no matter how hard one tries, just as in other activities. The best advice is not to force the situation. Just as an investor cuts back when the stock market is in a slump, a horseplayer on a losing streak should reduce wagers until things start picking up again.

The worst way to react to a losing streak is to fall for one of the progressive betting patterns recommended in the "get rich quick" systems. Most of these systems suggest doubling every wager until a winner comes along. This would mean that a bettor who started with a $2 bet would find himself placing a $1,024 wager for the tenth race during a modest losing streak. I'm sorry, but to my way of thinking, progression systems are a sure path to the poorhouse. It's like the guy who needs to make payroll on Monday and is 5 percent short, so he goes to the track and bets on the favorite in the feature race expecting to get at least a 5 percent return on his investment. But when his horse runs fourth, he sees no alternative but to jump off a bridge. The term "bridge jumping" has become part of racing jargon, but it will probably never become as popular as the term "upset." This incidentally came about as a result of a horse named Upset beating the horse of the people, Secretariat, in the 1973 Whitney Stake, and sports wags have used the term to death.

Earlier I said I would give you a book for true speed handicappers, however, I decided to do you one better.

When I first heard about Randy Moss and his program called Pace Figures, I thought that he was just making another tool to be sold by the *Daily Racing Form*, so I put the program specs aside like other junk mail. I must admit, however, that I do like Randy Moss, and I said to myself, "Let's give it a try." Conceptually, it requires a more detailed look at individual horses in a given race and can best be described as an enhancement to the race figures currently in the past performance sheets.

For those of you who are kindly described as members of racing's geek squad, I offer the following: Twenty-first century technology can be accused of expanding the information superhighway to the farthest reaches of the earth. So much data is traveling in microseconds or even at warp speed through cyberspace; in many cases, there is no cost to the consumer.

Notwithstanding the advantages and pleasure of seeing the world shrink to the size of a lady's thong, the question that comes to mind is whether this easy dissemination of information also is shrinking the pari-mutuel handle at many racetracks. The freewheeling and haphazard distribution of the live signal of racing programs to almost any enterprising individual who wishes to book gambling on horses has spawned an offshore industry filled with the possibility of some form of defalcation.

The thieves may be mere pickpockets compared to the Caribbean pirates of the eighteenth century, but there are a lot of them.

The legitimate offshore operations that accept wagering on Thoroughbred racing and contract with North American tracks to do so are extremely profitable. They offer an alternative to attending a live racing program by providing a means of in-home wagering on races at almost any racetrack of the bettor's choice.

It is unclear how detrimental on-track wagering has become to this industry, but the growth in the handle has been spectacular. Naively being regarded as "new-found money," most tracks are prepared to sell their signal for a mere 4 percent to 6 percent of their handle.

The revenue to operators of books throughout the Caribbean, as well in South and Central America, that do not have contracts with racetracks is unknown, and the return to the tracks is absolutely nothing; but, collectively, it may be significant. And if it comes largely from betting by natives of the respective countries and tourists, as some would believe, it would be new-found money.

Realistically, the term new-found money in this case is a euphemism for the newest form of laundering currency from drug proceeds. And it's probably on a scale that would give the Maytag repairman something else to do.

It appears that little has been done to prevent the siphoning-off of wagering revenue or to collect from unlicensed operations. This is because the racing industry is facilitating the pirates rather than impeding them. Tracks that have their live-racing broadcast by such networks as Television Games Network (TVG) and past performances available through Internet distribution of the *Daily Racing Form* and Equibase are being exploited without compensation from these bootleggers.

St. Maarten and many other Caribbean islands are named for saints but, ironically, they have no shortage of thieves. On a recent Monday, a facility known as the Lightning Casino in St. Maarten blatantly accepted wagering supported by a TVG broadcast shown on monitors throughout its premises.

When attempting to photograph the operation, I was thrown out on the street, but not before being permitted to buy an exacta. The casino pays track odds, which means, of course, it receives the same takeout as the track, without its overhead. Obviously, these operations have to handle only a fraction of what a track would require to be just as profitable. It is noteworthy that the Lightning Casino is presently going through an extensive expansion.

Is there is a watchdog for North American tracks? If so, it appears to be Stevenson & Associates (S&A), which acts as an agent in contracting with approximately twenty-five North American tracks and legitimate offshore betting facilities in sixteen countries and territories. On numerous occasions, S&A has reported signal theft to unsuspecting tracks, most recently Lone Star Park and River Downs. Since its inception, S&A has produced evidence of the signal being pirated in Trinidad, Antigua, St. Maarten, the Dominican Republic, Argentina, Juarez, and eighteen additional locations in Mexico.

"To protect our tracks," said S&A president David Stevenson, "S&A encrypts all racing data and supplies it only to the wagering facilities that have a contract for the signal; and to protect all tracks, we are attempting to persuade Equibase to do the same. So far, they have objected to this policy."

Chris Scherf, executive vice president of the Thoroughbred Racing Association, believes that the books that are not contracted with North American tracks are not a major concern.

"These operations are generally small," he contended. "They will not accept large bets, and they limit payoffs on exotics. Only the larger operations like William Hill and Ladbrokes can afford to take that risk. The problem, however, is with rebating by the books that can take large bets because they're merging their wagers into the U.S. pari-mutuel pools. They are in competition with the tracks."

One legitimate offshore telephone account wagering facility is Racing and Gaming Services (RGS), based on the island of St. Kitts. They contract mainly through the services of S&A with many of the North American Thoroughbred and greyhound tracks. RGS is now a major offshore wagering facility; its handle is estimated to be $200 million a year.

"To protect a track from loss of attendance and on-track wagering, S&A's contract with us prohibits accepting bets from clients within the state of the host track," said Kirk Brooks, President and CEO of RGS. "In addition, bets are only accepted from individuals who are screened carefully and have established an account by submitting a Social Security number, personal identification photograph, and an established residence."

RGS is perhaps also unique in that its clients, who are invariably high-stake bettors, are almost exclusively shareholders in the company.

"This effectively removes any expectation our clients might have of receiving rebates, which are invariably offered at casinos and even at some racetracks," Brooks said. "Our company was formed by a consortium of high-stake gamblers who objected to the high takeout prevalent in the racing industry. They wanted to reduce the effect of this by becoming shareholders."

To compete with casinos that offer rebates, some tracks feel compelled to do the same for their prime customers. Perhaps more advantageous would be following RGS's example and, rather than rebates, offer stock in the track as an incentive to major punters. From a bettor's point of view, however, rebates and stock options are often a "rose by any other name."

Bets are placed with RGS by calling a toll-free number and being connected through a hub in Birmingham, Alabama. "A hub is necessary for a single line connection," Brooks said. "It would not be practical to communicate with each individual track and client directly from St. Kitts."

The facility in St. Kitts operates out of a single room with approximately thirty telephone operators placed in individual booths, each with a computer terminal. In view of the operators is a bank of television monitors, each displaying live broadcasts from the host tracks on which they accept wagering. Pre-race odds, payoffs, and instant race results are immediately available to operators and clients online. A sophisticated recording device provides a backup of all transactions and can be used to settle any disputes. Outside of the building is an array of satellite antenna dishes connected to decoders within the building, which unscramble the signal from each track.

St. Kitts does not have a racing industry that can be impacted by such offshore wagering facilities as RGS, but by importing racing signals, bookmakers in Trinidad have deprived the local racetrack of sufficient revenue, thereby contributing to its bankruptcy. It is only through its government's intervention that the track is going to survive. The four principle bookmakers who have legitimately contracted with North American tracks through S&A have negotiated an arrangement with the government to protect the local racing industry. It is obvious, at least there, that wagering on racing from outside of Trinidad has had sufficient economic impact to necessitate protection for their own racing.

Similar problems exist in Jamaica, where it is estimated that there are approximately 400 illegal books that take about 50 percent of the potential revenue from the track; in 1990 it was driven into receivership. In some of the Caribbean countries, residents of the island are not allowed into casinos, so there is not much income lost to their tracks from local bettors.

The casinos and bookmakers, however, whether legal or not, stay profitable by receiving much of their income from offering gambling to tourists and North American bettors. Until the states provide legal telephone account wagering, the loss of income to the racing industry is enormous.

California has recently legalized full-blown casinos on Indian reservations, without limitations concerning their proximity to racetracks and with a total disregard for the potentially crippling economic drains on the racing industry. If anything can be learned from the experience of the tracks in Trinidad and Jamaica, it has certainly not registered with California legislators. In this sense, Indian casinos and Caribbean bookies may well be synonymous. The loss in revenue from wagering going out of state and offshore, exacerbated by the proliferation of Indian casinos, is a compelling reason for even the most myopic legislator to promote the legalization of telephone account and Internet wagering.

In closing, I'd like to leave you with a story of what happens when people start to forget about the *small tracks* around the country. It's the sum and substance of what really makes the sport. It's the story of Penn National.

The Penn National Race Course sits nestled at the foot of the Blue Ridge Mountains of central Pennsylvania in the central blue-collar town of Grantville. Grantville is a place where most of the local economy is derived from farms and local businesses; it's a location that depends on Thoroughbred racing year-round—exactly 210 days yearly. It is the kind of racing and wagering that makes small-town America more than just a Norman Rockwell painting. It's the place where a $250 profit at the end of a night means an extra pair of jeans for your son, something pretty for your daughter, and maybe even a better cut of meat on the table. It's the kind of place where a fairly good streak of winners can bring a moment of excitement to a man. The kind of excitement that lets him introduce his lifetime partner of some ten years or more as his bride. Sure the years and the children have added a few pounds around her, just like they've changed his flowing mane to a collective wisp of follicles that seem to only fall where he wants them to when in the shower.

Much of Penn National's labor force are permanent, hard-working folk. There are dozens of residents employed on the backstretch and on the frontside. They work as parimutuel clerks, security, food service help, and track maintenance. And, of course, there are jockeys, owners, and trainers, without whom there would be no racing.

The 2000 season, however, saw a scandal that cut deeper than the deep planting necessary to hold the roots of the rhubarb. The working-class nighttime race track, located about 10 miles from the famous Hershey Chocolate Factory and Amusement Park, was shaken by the knowledge that, for the second time in its twenty-eight-year history, a race-fixing scandal had reared its head.

Years before, back in 1984, seven jockeys were arrested in a sting operation by the Pennsylvania Attorney General's Office. But locals said that it was the strangest thing that they had ever seen or heard of. It seemed that an undercover agent had offered $1,000 to the jockeys to fix a race, but no races actually were fixed. And if that wasn't odd enough, five of the jockeys involved pleaded guilty and two were convicted of conspiracy.

Then, some sixteen years later, even more lives and careers were ruined and the track's reputation sullied worse than before. This time, the plot was the brainchild of a pair of horse owners who appeared to have seen the movie *Goodfellas* and decided that they could do "Hollywood" one better.

This time the stake was even lower for the seven implicated jockeys, six of whom pleaded guilty in U.S. District Court in Harrisburg; the charge was one count each of bribery for fixing a sporting contest, which is a federal felony. The maximum penalties are five years in federal prison and a $250,000 fine for each count. A plea bargain deal, however, brought the pinky-ringed defendants no more than a slap on the wrist in the form of probation and a modest fine. This time, the plot twist called for most of the accused riders to testify against the lone jockey who had pleaded not guilty. His name was Felix Pinero.

The case proceeded to a jury trial in January 2001. In a plot turn that you would think only happens in Los Angeles, Pinero was acquitted of all charges. Why? It appeared that the government's witnesses so ticked off the jury that they could not or, should I say, wouldn't find him guilty. And as payment for their stellar testimony, the federal prosecutors decided to honor the plea bargains. And once again the Feds pitched a "no hitter."

Jockeys Lazaro Vives, Ramon Pena, Luis Morales, Rocky Jurado, and Andres Reyes all received their lightened sentences later that year, with each amounting to no more than an intentional walk, although it's likely they may never be licensed to compete on a U.S. racetrack again. Manuel Torres, whom Penn National trainers labeled "the most notorious" of the race-fixers, is hiding in Panama as a fugitive; the FBI is still attempting to haul him back to Pennsylvania to face the music.

But the lingering effects of the scandal left a skunk-like stench on every aspect of this small but tight racing community—from the trainers, grooms, and hot walkers, all the way up through the management of Penn National Gaming Corp.

According to court records, Vives was paid $2,100 to fix a total of three Thoroughbred races; Jurado and Reyes accepted $1,400 in bribes to fix two races each, and Torres faced two counts of taking $1,000 to throw two races. These events occurred between January and May 2000, with up to 15 incidents cited. Penn National trainers felt there were many more race-fixing instances that went undetected.

Owners George Berryhill, seventy, of Lebanon, Pennsylvania, and Neil McElwee, forty-five, of Harrisburg, Pa. were the so-called "masterminds" behind the scheme, utilizing jockey Pena as their mule, instructor, and paymaster. McElwee and Berryhill, as partners, owned several horses stabled on the Penn National grounds, and while some thought the pair could never plan this type of scheme, other trainers were not surprised.

But one of the most convenient comments came from trainer John Zimmerman. "They were big gamblers. You know gamblers dream of doing things like that," said Zimmerman, whose horse Fortyeight Braves lost as a prohibitive favorite on February 25 when Vives fell off his mount. The Equibase chart of the race stated Vives fell off Fortyeight Braves for "no apparent reason." To keep the horse off the board, Vives accepted the princely sum of $700, while Berryhill and McElwee allegedly loaded up on trifecta tickets that did not include the 2-to-1 favorite.

Later the journeyman jockey testified under oath during the Felix Pinero trial that he earned approximately $70,000 riding at Penn National in 2000; of course, bribes were not included.

"Laz said he lost an iron and I truly did believe him," Zimmerman said. "The kid won a ton of races for me and I said to myself, 'No, he couldn't possibly do that.' I was blown away from it. These people were like family to me. I grew up with McElwee's family and was a pallbearer at a funeral. It hurts to think they'd do this. These guys all deserve whatever they get. They're gone for good, their lives and families are ruined and I don't feel sorry for any of them."

Clinton Potts, who was Penn National's leading rider in 2000, was watching the race from the jockeys' room when that particular incident occurred. Potts, who is recovering from cracked ribs, a broken arm, a broken leg, and sprained ankle sustained in a February 14 spill this year, recollected the specific race.

Potts said, "I had ridden this horse before and, in my opinion, there was no way the horse could get beat, unless something like that happened." He continued to say, "For the next couple of days after that, I busted on Laz and Zimmerman."

Potts said that there was "a lot of anguish" in the jockeys' room when the truth surfaced. "The same thing came out of everyone's mouth," said Potts. "'Can you believe it?'"

"There's no way I could have believed it. The only thing in my mind was that it may have been a confidence builder, just to see if they could get away with it, not for the amount of money involved."

Morales and Vives were two of the more successful jockeys in the colony. The others apparently were struggling to make a living.

In 1995 Vives appeared to have a bright future at his feet. He was the leading apprentice jockey at Monmouth Park for the second consecutive year, finishing fifth behind noted journeymen Joe Bravo,

Rick Wilson, and the now-retired Herb McCauley in the overall rider standings, posting 46 victories in 327 starts, including a victory in that meeting's Continental Mile Stake.

Vives joined his brother, Juan, in Grantville after losing his apprentice allowance that autumn. Tragically, Juan was murdered in 1997, knifed to death after finding two men breaking into his automobile in front of his home.

"I'll tell you something, Juan was a straight guy. If he were still alive, he would have shot Laz himself," Zimmerman said.

Conversely, Vives is actually the only jockey to have won a race with a horse he was allegedly paid to have held back. Corporate Exec, a six-year-old Corporate Report gelding trained by Karen Kunes, won on March 24 after Vives supposedly accepted a $700 bribe to hold the horse back.

"You always hear things around the racetrack, but then you started seeing things that you could look at and see weren't kosher," said Kunes, one of Penn National's perennial top five conditioners. "He broke bad and was dead-last but still won," Kunes said. "He got claimed after that race and won three straight."

Other trainers also started seeing subtle, yet very apparent, signs on the racetrack that some Penn National races just weren't on the up-and-up.

Trainer Mary Cacchiotti, who trained 1999 Penn National Horse of the Year Special Dancer, was so furious over the ride Torres gave Outlaw Biker Stables' Personal Princess in March 2000 that she went straight to the stewards to vent and to request an investigation. This incident was not one of the counts mentioned in the indictment, but the conditioner recollected it as though it happened last week.

"(Torres) ran from me with his tack in his hands back to the jockeys' room like a dog, saying the horse was sore," she said. "I wanted to strangle the little #*$. I'm watching the race through binoculars, she's twenty lengths behind at three-to-five odds, and he's standing on his head to keep her from running. I put Clinton on the horse, and she won two in a row with him."

Cacchiotti approached the stewards and asked them to review the tape of that race. Shortly afterward, Don Anderson of the local Thoroughbred Racing Protective Bureau was forced to step in. "[General Manager] Richie [Schnarrs] called me and said he thought something was going on. I said I'd go after it with the state FBI. They have a lot more power than we do," Anderson said.

Schnarrs and Anderson gave their full cooperation to authorities. In September, when the indictments became public, Schnarrs stated publicly, "Our obligation is to ensure a fair and level playing field for all participants. That means the betting public, the owners, the trainers, and the jockeys who compete and make their livelihood here."

Chief Penn National steward Dean Nickerson declined to comment, citing an order from the Pennsylvania Department of Agriculture.

Ironically, a half-page advertisement now runs inside the daily track program, encouraging people "who suspect or know of any wrongdoing within the racing community," to phone a toll-free hotline, promising total confidentiality.

The attorneys for Vives (William Tully), McElwee (Robert Tarman), and Berryhill (Paul Killion) did not return phone calls. The remaining jockeys utilized court-appointed public defenders.

Pinero's January trial in front of Harrisburg U.S. District Court judge Yvette Kane illustrated just how badly conceived and unstructured the entire scheme was. Pinero was a religious man by all accounts and turned out to be the worst person to approach to take a bribe. "He was the most religious man I ever saw on the racetrack. He never uttered a cuss word," Potts said.

Pinero took out his apprentice license at New Hampshire's Rockingham Park in 1989 and was licensed in Pennsylvania, Delaware, New York, Maryland, and West Virginia. He told defense attorney Samuel Rivera under direct examination on January 12 that his total income of about $27,000, which supports his spouse and four children, was mainly derived from galloping horses at ten dollars per horse, since his conversion to Judaism in 1992.

Pinero refused to accept racing mounts on Friday nights and Saturdays, just as committed to his beliefs as Sandy Koufax was when he refused to pitch a World Series game on Yom Kippur for the Los Angeles Dodgers in the 1960s.

U.S. Assistant District Attorney William Behe grilled Pinero on the witness stand during a January 12, 2001 cross-examination about bribes of $1,000 offered to him to hold Big Hello and Pocket Picker off the board on May 6 and 7, 2000, respectively.

According to trial transcripts, however, Behe had very little hard evidence that could serve to implicate Pinero, except for the jockey's reluctance to talk with FBI agents for fear of being implicated; he refused to talk on three separate occasions.

Pinero told the jury that FBI agents approached him in August of last year, questioning him on whether he was involved in fixing races at Penn National or if he had knowledge about it. Pinero explained to the jury that he said nothing until being indicted for fear of being "arrested for something I didn't do."

"Mr. Pena came to me one time and threw $500 down on the sofa," Pinero testified during Behe's cross-examination. "[Pena] said, 'This is the way we are working here now. You got some people fixing races here and they want to fix these races.' I say, you know better. I don't work that way. I told him I don't want his money."

Behe continued unsuccessfully to try to cast doubt concerning Pinero's competence and effort for the last-place finish on Big Hello.

"I think the prosecution relied too heavily on Pena," Rivera said. "He even admitted at one point that he was testifying because his lawyer said he would avoid jail time. We consistently maintained that Pena implicated Felix because [Pena] was the one pocketing the money."

Rivera said the prosecution put Vives on the stand to attempt to illustrate why jockeys who were making a decent living might accept bribes. Vives testified that he was in dire financial straits, despite his earnings of $70,000 in 2000, which he stated was the reason he accepted the bribes.

"One of the things I asked the jury to think about was why a man with four children and a wife to support would jeopardize his career for $500 or $1,000,' Rivera said.

The remainder of the cross-examination was a slam-dunk for Pinero, despite the fact he doesn't speak much English. The prosecution questioned Pinero time and time again about employment of race strategy, Big Hello's problem with bolting, and a subsequent change of the bit for the May 6, 2000 race. "He don't have the speed to keep up with those kinds of horses that night," he testified. "I go inside to save ground."

Behe then asked Pinero to explain what "saving ground" and "asking" a horse meant.

"Mr. [Charles] DiMario [the trainer] told me to take him back, save ground, and ask him at the three-eighths pole. I started hitting the horse on the shoulder asking, but he don't respond," Pinero said.

Behe questioned Pinero that if he had been paid to keep the horse from winning, why he "put on such a show" by whipping Big Hello even though they were 19 to 20 lengths off the lead at the top of the stretch. Pinero told Behe that he "never accepted money to hold the horse" and cited Pennsylvania racing rules, which require horses to be ridden out throughout a race. Big Hello also finished last in his subsequent race.

"The prosecution never called DiMario to the witness stand," Rivera noted. Instead, they based its case on the testimony of the jockeys and a steward from Arizona who broke down tapes of the May 6, 2000 race, frame-by-frame.

Rivera called trainer Scott Lake to refute the testimony. Pinero had worked for Lake for several years as an exercise rider. Lake's testimony was unavailable from the U.S. district attorney clerk's office.

The prosecution sensed they were losing the case. Over several objections by defense counsel, Rivera began to grasp at straws. Behe hammered away at Pinero over four careless riding suspensions during his apprentice seasons at Rockingham, then tried to link him with a buzzer incident involving Victor Ramirez in 1996, and finally questioned his possible socialization with certain jockeys.

"Felix did a decent job. The prosecutors tried to shoot holes into his credibility by asking questions that were ancillary and had nothing to do with the case," Rivera said.

Behe pressed on. "Did you see these [other indicted jockeys] socially? Did you drink with them? Did you eat with them?" Pinero answered "no" each time.

"Did you give your best effort on Big Hello on May 6?" Behe asked.

"Yes, sir," was Pinero's reply, ending the cross-examination. Pinero's testimony on cross-examination, combined with the fact that he rode Pocket Picker to a second-place finish the following evening, was enough for the jury to acquit him. "There were too many inconsistencies in the testimony of Pena and Vives and the jury saw right through that," Rivera said.

Pinero, who galloped horses for Lake in the past, is doing so again in Maryland now, according to Rivera. "I don't think this adversely affected Felix at all. He was exonerated; he'll apply to get his jockey's license back and move on. I do think it adversely affected the integrity of the entire jockey colony of Penn National," Rivera said.

The recovery process for the Penn National racing community has begun slowly, but the early results are better on the frontside than on the backstretch. The track, like so many others across the United States, depends on dollars wagered off-track and out-of-state on its live product for its purse survival. It also depends heavily on wagering from signals it imports.

Typically, Penn National handles between $60,000 and $80,000 per night on track, according to figures provided by Equibase. The bulk of wagering is derived from its exported simulcast signal, which was averaging approximately $1 million per night earlier this year. Its nighttime Thoroughbred signal is year-round, and in the winter, it doesn't get much competition at northeast simulcast outlets. In Las Vegas, its signal hits the racebooks at 4:20 p.m. Pacific Time.

"We're on the way back," Schnarrs said. "The off-track handle is creeping up towards $1.2 million a night once again." As Schnarrs spoke, a four-horse field approached the wire with jockey Pedro Carrasquel whipping and driving three-year-old Ms. Cappucio hard along the rail to miss gaining the show spot by a nose.

"That's been the case now ever since this happened. The racing is clean," Schnarrs said.

Penn National's purse distribution on March 8 was $68,900 for a nine-race card that consisted of two allowance races, a starter's allowance, two maiden claiming races, and claiming races for tags of $3,500, $5,000, and $12,500. Yet, on that early March evening, its expansive Mountain View Dining Room was deserted except for five occupied tables. Track announcer John Bogar's voice echoed several times off the walls of the nearly deserted clubhouse.

Parent company Penn National Gaming, under the direction of William Bork, knows what it takes to get people into the track. The company operates six off-track wagering sites under its Penn National license. It also owns the Downs at Pocono, a harness track in Wilkes-Barre, and its four off-track wagering sites. It is a part-owner of Freehold Raceway, another harness track in central New Jersey. The "crown jewel" is West Virginia's Charles Town Races, where more than a thousand video slot machines, in addition to simulcasting and live racing, is the straw that stirs the corporate drink.

Public perception still needs work. One player concentrating on out-of-town races, with a beer in one hand and a *Daily Racing Form* spread out on a bar table, admitted he never wagers on Penn National races. "Since I live twenty minutes away. I come here to play the bigger tracks. I can't figure out what's going here," said the middle-aged man who declined to give his name. Yet, a portion of every dollar the gentleman wagers benefits Penn National purses.

Backstretchers still haven't fully recovered from the events of early 2000. The wounds and doubt remain in spite of the financial recovery.

"I think it hurt racing all over, not just here," Potts said. "When the story came out, people I do business with in Maryland said that handle went down there as well. It was a temporary black cloud that hurt racing."

Potts said he was planning to move his track from Grantville to Delaware Park this spring, but that his injuries have changed those plans. He still intends, however, to pursue them once he is healed and fit.

Penn National is a place where trainers do much of the "hands-on" work by themselves. There are no people named Mott, Baffert, Jerkens, or Lukas who can delegate authority to staff. Many exercise their own horses and join in the back-breaking manual labor. There's no warm and cozy place to watch workouts on a cold March morning with its piercing wind. Trainers drive their vehicles to the top of a hill and view the proceedings through binoculars.

Cacchiotti said the scandal "hurt this place really bad. We work hard to put on the show here. When a horse doesn't run right because it's held, we're spending money calling the vets to see if something is wrong. I know one guy owned a bar and another worked for a utility company. These were no ingenious people. Something has to be done," she said.

Trainers with options are planning to act upon them. "I have fifty-two horses here and fifteen on the farm. I'm going to take a string of thirty out of Delaware Park in the spring," Zimmerman said. "I know there are going to be a lot of fresh horses there, but with the slots, the purses are bigger."

There will always be a horse population at Penn National since bottom-level allowances and claimers need a place to compete for what really is a pretty decent purse structure.

Still, two strikes from two scandals in sixteen years have forced management, horsemen, and jockeys into a position where they must protect home plate and avoid a fateful third strike.

Acknowledgments

I WISH TO THANK:

The public relations and marketing departments of the tracks mentioned in this book for providing me with track programs, conditioning books, and other invaluable information.

They are:
- ♣ Finger Lakes
- ♣ Great Lakes Downs
- ♣ Lone Star Park
- ♣ Turf Paradise
- ♣ Tampa Bay Downs
- ♣ Turfway Park

The management of Finger Lakes Racetrack for the intimate exposure to racing; and the racing people, who were critical in sharpening this book.

The Public Relations Department of Great Lakes Downs and particularly Executive Assistant Chrissy Dailey, who understands rapid turn around.

The Daily Racing Form for its great coverage of the Sport of Kings.

The NYRA staff and also their media guides, which often pointed me in the right direction and gave historical clarity to my sometimes-foggy memory.

Bert Randolph Sugar, the world's greatest historian on boxing, who showed me clearness and determination.

Dave Johnson, a great announcer and super fact finder.

The late Jim Murray, whose writings on California racing gave me a deeper understanding of West Coast racing.

The late Joseph H. Palmer, in particular for his book entitled *This Was Racing*. It's my Bible.

The publication *The Complete Book of Thoroughbred Horse Racing* and its authors, Tom Biracree and Wendy Insinger, who made fact finding an art.

To the patrons and cashiers at the OTB parlor at Seventh Avenue and Thirty-eighth Street, New York City.

The archives of *The Blood-Horse Magazine*.

Equibase, and in particular, Shelby Cook, who helped me when I kept forgetting my password.

The publication *Backstretch Magazine*, and writers like John Russell, who had great insight into offshore Internet betting parlors as well as the travesties that nearly whistled the demise of Penn National.

Mark Weinstein, who knows that sports is more than a game—it's a passion.

Trish Hoard, who reminded me that a *Dangling Participle* is more than a race horse.

Warren "Silver Fox" Fisher, who could spot an overlay at any track in America, RIP.

All of the credit for accuracy should be given to those mentioned above; the errors are sadly my own.